601
Great Scrapbook Ideas

601

Great Scrapbook Ideas

From the editors of Memory Makers Books

Memory Makers Books
Cincinnati, Ohio
www.memorymakersmagazine.com

PB: 12 11 10 09 08   5 4 3 2 1
PLC: 12 11 10 09 08   5 4 3 2 1

Distributed in Canada by Fraser Direct
100 Armstrong Avenue
Georgetown, ON, Canada L7G 5S4
Tel: (905) 877-4411

Distributed in the U.K. and Europe by David & Charles
Brunel House, Newton Abbot, Devon, TQ12 4PU, England
Tel: (+44) 1626 323200, Fax: (+44) 1626 323319
E-mail: postmaster@davidandcharles.co.uk

Distributed in Australia by Capricorn Link
P.O. Box 704, S. Windsor, NSW 2756 Australia
Tel: (02) 4577-3555

Library of Congress Cataloging-in-Publication Data
601 great scrapbook ideas / editors of Memory Makers Books.
     p. cm.
  Includes index.
  ISBN 978-1-59963-017-5 (pbk. : alk. paper)
  ISBN 978-1-59963-037-3 (hardcover : alk. paper)
 1. Paper work. 2. Scrapbooks. I. Memory Makers Books. II. Title: Six hundred and one great scrapbook ideas.
TT870.A16 2007
745.593--dc22

2007029074

fw
F+W PUBLICATIONS, INC.
www.fwpublications.com

Editor: **Christine Doyle**
Designer: **Kelly O'Dell**
Writer: **Courtney Walsh**
Art Coordinator: **Eileen Aber**
Production Coordinator: **Matt Wagner**
Photographers: **Al Parrish, Kris Kandler, Robert Best**

A Note from the Editor

In your hands is the work of hundreds of scrapbook artists. Hundreds of people, many just like you, who created a layout (or several) that they are really proud of. Artists who wanted to share their work and their love of scrapbooking with you.

How did we here at Memory Makers Books get all these fantastic layouts? Well, we asked. We asked readers of our Web site and our e-newsletter to send images of their favorite layouts. And from there, the word spread. To other online message boards, to blogs and more. Almost instantly, the e-mails came pouring in. E-mails filled with images of layouts created by people who love scrapbooking.

Three of us on the books staff worked on sorting the e-mails, all the while selecting a diverse group of layouts to feature in this book. Each layout was selected for a variety of reasons: because it had a great photo, or a compelling story or an inspiring design. We selected layouts that came from artists all over the world. We selected layouts featuring kids, and husbands, vacations and holidays. And although we weren't able to publish all of the thousands of entries we received, we thoroughly enjoyed looking at and reading every single one.

So to all the amazing contributors to this book—thank you. Thank you for sharing your layouts with us and for inspiring us to create our own great scrapbook pages.

Enjoy!

Christine Doyle
Executive Editor, Memory Makers Books
F+W Publications, Inc.

Table of Contents

Introduction 9

1 everyday Life 10

Ideas to record the moments that make up every day, from chill time to bedtime and everything in between.

2 HARD *to* FORGET 50

Holidays, events, seasons of sun and snow—ways to recall those memories you never really forget.

3 More than a *Princess* 102

From princess skirts to soccer balls, tons of ways to show off girls made of more than just sugar and spice.

4 More than Prince Charming — 156

Inspiration for scrapbooking the men in your life, whether they're playing sports, digging up dirt, or flashing you a mischievous smile.

5 Open Heart — 204

Ideas for truly capturing the family ties and friendships that make you who you are.

Source Guide 266

Index of Contributors 269

Index 271

Introduction

Inspiration. Motivation. Ideas. We all need them. We need them in just about every facet of our lives and scrapbooking is no exception. We all hit those creative roadblocks that make it frustrating to try and go on. We can't think of a great page idea, or a creative design or a new technique to try to bring the joy back into the hobby we love.

Enter *601 Great Scrapbook Ideas*. With this book in your creative arsenal, you'll never run out of inspiration for your layouts. While working on this book, I was struck by so many great ideas are represented here. Gorgeous pages and interesting new techniques equal a whole lot of eye candy and loads of fun! Once you leaf through this idea book, it's likely you'll want to run to your scrapbook table and get started on several new projects.

This book will challenge you to try new things, show you how to do techniques you've always wanted to try and give you page ideas you'll want to remember. With a variety of scrapbookers included in this book, there's a tremendous amount of variation in style and voice. You will love having this book on your shelf, but it's unlikely it will stay there for very long. Chances are, you'll be pulling it down time and time again when that creative rut strikes.

So, sit back and enjoy these 601 glorious scrapbooking ideas! I think you just might love every page.

Courtney Walsh
Writer, scrapbook designer, and author

chapter

everyday Life

A sweet glance. A cold milkshake. A child fast asleep on the couch.
All are simple things, and simple things can mean so much.
It's the nitty gritty moments in between special events that make
life worth living. It's easy to take for granted the mundane "stuff
of life," assuming there's no way we could ever forget our hopes for
our children or the wild and crazy haircut our toddlers are sporting.
Unfortunately, though, these memories will fade, leaving only the
photographs as evidence. Let this chapter inspire you to capture those
simple memories that strike a chord with you today. Years from now,
when you look back, you will have documented evidence of the real
life you lived... and if you're really brave, you may even include
some of the not-so-pretty stuff too!

Great Scrapbook Idea!

Odds are, if you're like most scrapbookers you've got piles of scraps all over your space! Instead of shoveling them into the garbage, why not turn your trash into scrapbook gold? Jennifer's layout is a wonderful example of some of the fun ways you can incorporate scraps onto your next layout. Why not try product packaging, the negative space on an empty sheet of stickers or the scratch sheet that served as a paint barrier between your desk and your last masterpiece?

Paperaholic

Jennifer Armentrout
Lynchburg, Virginia

Supplies: Patterned paper (BasicGrey, Cosmo Cricket, My Mind's Eye, K&Co., Rusty Pickle); chipboard letters (Bazzill, Heidi Swapp, Making Memories); acrylic paint; notebook paper; newspaper; ticket stubs; staples; hole punch; sandpaper; pen

My Turn

Annemarie Mackin
Safety Harbor, Florida

Supplies: Cardstock; patterned paper (Imagination Project); rhinestones, velvet letter stickers (Making Memories); flowers (Bazzill, Heidi Swapp); flower punch (EK Success); circle punch; brads

Nicole Harper
Elyria, Ohio

Supplies: Cardstock; patterned paper (BasicGrey, FontWerks, SEI); decorative tape (7gypsies); letter stickers (7gypsies, American Crafts, Doodlebug, EK Success, Heidi Grace, Urban Lily); rub-on letters (American Crafts, Making Memories); rhinestones; acrylic paint; staples; pen

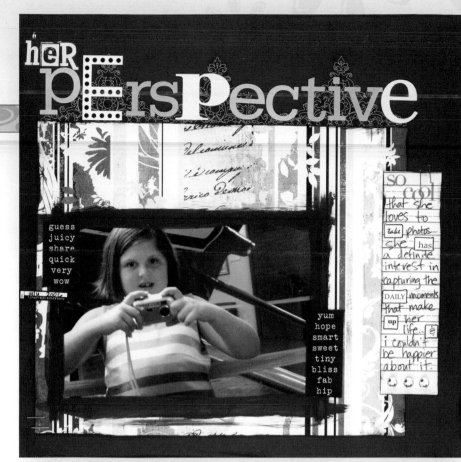

Capturing Color

Paola López-Araiza Osante
Mexico City, Mexico

Supplies: Patterned paper (BasicGrey); puzzle pieces (Rusty Pickle); chipboard letters (Heidi Swapp); rickrack (Li'l Davis); acrylic paint; thread

Great Scrapbook Idea!

For a great three-dimensional effect, consider matting your photos on stray puzzle pieces. By distressing the edges, Paola was able to keep the focus on the point of the layout—the color.

This technique of "washing out" the rest of the layout to make the intended focal point pop works great no matter what you want to highlight.

Gone

Sara Dickey
Richmond, Virginia

Supplies: Cardstock; patterned paper (American Crafts, My Mind's Eye); chipboard letters (Heidi Swapp); rub-on accents (BasicGrey); pigment ink; pen

Gone are the days of the sweetly posed group shot. Now it is all about making goofy faces.
-Charlotte, Carter & Jack 3-07

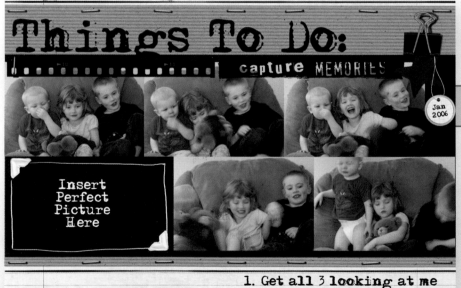

Things to Do

Kim Christensen
Fair Oaks, California

Supplies: Digital clip, film strip, paper, tag (Digital Design Essentials); felt star (LilyPad); photo corners (CD Muckosky); Adler font (Internet download)

Things To Do:
capture MEMORIES

Jan 2006

Insert Perfect Picture Here

1. Get all 3 looking at me
2. No tickling
3. Have everyone smiling
4. All sitting still
5. Eyes Open
6. Just give up.
7. Realize these are perfect.

Great Scrapbook Idea!

Taking photos under the oh-so-flattering bathroom lights may not produce the most ideal results. If you're caught with orange-tinted, washed-out photos, don't discard them, convert them! By changing her low-light photos to black and white, Kelly was able to salvage these adorable pictures, complementing them with whatever color she wanted!

Later Gator

Kelly Bryan
Avon Lake, Ohio

Supplies: Cardstock; letter accents and stickers, patterned paper (American Crafts); journaling card (FontWerks); date sticker (7gypsies); word stickers (EK Success); photo corners; pen

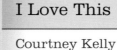

I Love This

Courtney Kelly
Anchorage, Alaska

Supplies: Cardstock; buttons, patterned paper (American Crafts); letter stickers (Doodlebug, EK Success)

Freckles

Staci Compher
Carleton, Michigan

Supplies: Cardstock; die-cut accents, patterned paper (Fancy Pants); chipboard letters (Making Memories); patterned transparency (My Mind's Eye); pen

pajamas & cocoa puffs

It's a scene I've seen 100 times before. Nothing new...nothing really special... but this photo touches my heart. Why? Well, I'll tell you. Birthdays and holidays are important and well worth documenting. But by far, the moments I want to remember are moments like this. These simple moments that make up the core of our lives. I love to watch Skyler and how he spills half his cereal before it reaches his mouth. And I love the careful and successful way you pour your own milk. It's such a privilege to be your mother...to watch you grow and learn...to be a witness to these everyday simple moments.

Great Scrapbook Idea!

The next time you have a photo with a busy focal point, remember this sure fire way to keep the attention where you want it to be. Deena's layout is mostly dark, with just a few key elements highlighted, including the two children in her photo. By utilizing the center of the digital clock element, she was able to draw the eye directly onto the simple moment that touched her heart.

Simple Moments

Deena Wuest
Goessel, Kansas

Supplies: Digital elements (Designer Digitals); image editing software (Adobe); Avant Garde, Microgamma fonts (Internet download)

Anticipation

Maria Burke
Steinbach, Manitoba, Canada

Supplies: Cardstock; patterned paper (7gypsies, Creative Imaginations, Die Cuts With A View, SEI); letter stickers, round sticker (SEI); rub-on accents (Die Cuts With A View, SEI)

everyday when it gets close to lunchtime you go sit

in front of the door or watch by the window with great

anticipation waiting for Sarah to come home from preschool

as soon as you see her you run to the door squealing

with your arms open, waiting for a hug from your sister

Anna 11/06

Play Play Play

Krista L. Austin
Chicago, Illinois

Supplies: Cardstock; patterned paper, rub-on accents (Junkitz); patterned transparency (Creative Imaginations); dimensional adhesive; pen

Found It

Sarah van Wijck
Avalon Beach, New South Wales,
Australia

Supplies: Cardstock; patterned paper, rub-on letters (Scenic Route); ribbon (American Crafts, BasicGrey); stamp (Heidi Swapp); sticker accent (Creative Imaginations); staple; pen

Great Scrapbook Idea!

While Sandra's collage of photos was created digitally, you can easily create a similar look simply by cutting a photo and matting it with white cardstock. Then reassemble the photo in a somewhat staggered manner. This will create visual interest on your layout.

Not So Big

Sandra Stanton
Northfield, New Jersey

Supplies: Digital page kit, buttons (Agnes Lahur); letter stamp (Sweet Shoppe); curled edge (Designer Digitals); beaded trim, ribbon (Lilypad); shadow actions (Traci Murphy)

Jibby Jibby Ja

Alison Lockett
Knoxville, Tennessee

Supplies: Cardstock; patterned paper (A2Z); letter stickers (American Crafts); rub-on accents (Fancy Pants); stamp (Autumn Leaves); arrow accent (Scenic Route); pen

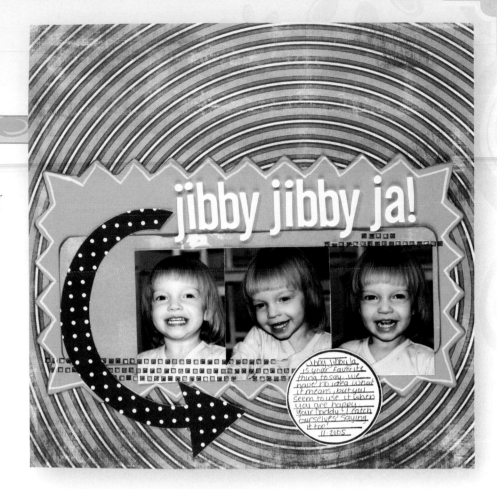

PARLE MOI...

Voilà plusieurs mois que tu as développé ton propre jargon. Tu t'exprimes continuellement du lever au coucher et souvent avec beaucoup d'affirmation, quand d'autres enfants plus âgés restent silencieux.

Cela nous ravit même si je trouve frustrant de ne pas te comprendre !

J'essaie, comme je l'ai lu, de te désigner chaque chose par son nom pour que tu le mémorises mais pour l'heure je ne reconnais aucun de ces mots dans ta bouche !

Je me demande souvent comment et à quel moment tu vas passer de cette succession de syllabes au français.

Tu es si coquine que j'imagine déjà avec délice les expressions les plus singulières que tu vas nous offrir.

Je n'en oublierai pas pour autant les "TADAD" qui font ton langage d'aujourd'hui.

Parle Moi

Champagne Severine
Dolomieu, France

Supplies: Digital cardstock, ribbon (Shabby Princess); digital patterned paper (Atomic Cupcake); brush (Magic Box); image editing software (Adobe)

11 février 07

19

flushed

away...
the fate of Sophia's
first lost tooth.

Sophia's Tooth Fairy was an inexperienced and forgetful one, having to slip her some cash at the last minute. (which, incidentally, he stole from her brother's piggy bank...) Little did Mommy know, however, that the Tooth Fairy wouldn't just TAKE the tooth, he would FLUSH the tooth down the toilet. Now, maybe it was silly to want to hold onto the first lost tooth. The Tooth Fairy certainly thought so. "It's a tooth," he said, matter-of-factly. "But it's the FIRST tooth!" Mommy retorted. "Yeah, but it's still a tooth." It was a losing battle. No sense in fighting. The tooth was gone... only to be remembered by the big gap in Sophia's gums and this photo. Mommy will have words with the Tooth Fairy before the second tooth falls out! February, 2007

Great Scrapbook Idea!

The next time someone in your family hits a milestone, go a little deeper than "just the facts" with your journaling. Think about some of the humorous or heartfelt aspects of a story that might be of interest to future generations. Resist the temptation to simply record what happened without telling how it happened and how you reacted to it. In the details is where you'll find the good stuff.

Flushed Away

Courtney Walsh
Winnebago, Illinois

Supplies: Digital paper kits (Two Peas in a Bucket); stitches (Shabby Princess); Century Gothic font (Microsoft)

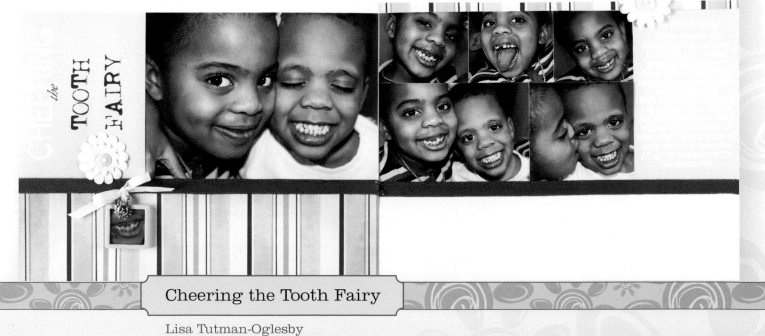

Cheering the Tooth Fairy

Lisa Tutman-Oglesby
Mundelein, Illinois

Supplies: Cardstock; button, flower, patterned paper (Making Memories); ribbon (Jo-Ann's); metal frame (Pebbles); charm (unknown); thread

Happy Feet

Edith van den Ordel
Lake Forest, California

Supplies: Cardstock; patterned paper (American Crafts); die-cut letters (Sizzix); rub-on letters, snaps (Making Memories); arrow accent (Microsoft); dimensional adhesive

They move in every direction.
They dance like there is no tomorrow.
They march to the beat of their own drum.
They are always facing forward; they never look back.
They are my daughter's feet, and very happy feet at that.

Play

Lisa Cloud
Sioux City, Iowa

Supplies: Patterned paper (BamPop, Chatterbox); scalloped placemat (Zingboom); chipboard accent (Imagination Project); rub-on letters (Li'l Davis); rickrack; pen

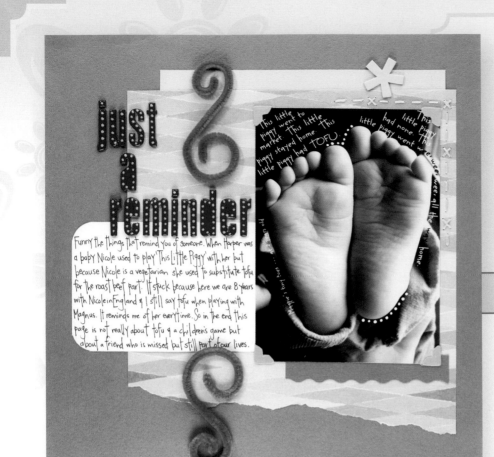

Great Scrapbook Idea!

Pipe cleaners aren't just for kids' crafts anymore! Take a cue from Crystal and raid your children's craft bins. Foam pieces, pipe cleaners even yarn would all make interesting additions to your next scrapbook page. You might even consider getting your kids in on the fun—they'll love creating unique projects from their own stash!

Just a Reminder

Crystal Jeffrey Rieger
Woodbridge, Ontario, Canada

Supplies: Cardstock; patterned paper (Paperwhite Memories); chipboard letters and shape, photo corners (Heidi Swapp); pipe cleaner; corner rounder; decorative scissors; floss; glossy topcoat (Ranger); image editing software (Adobe); pen

This Girl is Lucky

Nicole Harper
Elyria, Ohio

Supplies: Cardstock; patterned paper (FontWerks); rub-ons (CherryArte, Hambly); decorative tape, stamp, sticker accents (7gypsies); letter stickers (American Crafts); staples; pen

Ben pre-raincut 11-6-06

Great Scrapbook Idea!

Some scrapbooking tools don't necessarily have to be used the same way every time. On this layout, instead of the typical straight lines, Jennifer was able to create wild stitches, leaving them free to mimic her son's crazy hair. The next time you're using a tool, consider how you could manipulate it to convey a different message. You might love the results!

You Need a Cut

Jennifer Armentrout
Lynchburg, Virginia

Supplies: Cardstock; patterned paper (American Crafts, BasicGrey, My Mind's Eye); letter stickers (BasicGrey); stamps (Technique Tuesday); stamping ink; thread; pen

Rubber Chicken

Amy Hummel
St. George, Utah

Supplies: Cardstock; patterned paper (Chatterbox, Piggy Tales, Sassafras Lass, Scenic Route); letter stickers (American Crafts); rub-on accents (BasicGrey, Die Cuts With A View); stamps (7gypsies, Autumn Leaves); chipboard star (Heidi Swapp); brad; pen

Yum

Cindy Tobey
Kentwood, Michigan

Supplies: Chipboard letters, patterned paper, ribbon (We R Memory Keepers); letter stickers (EK Success); terry cloth trim (Rusty Pickle); foam stamps (Heidi Swapp); mesh (Magic Mesh); acrylic paint; pigment ink; buttons (Autumn Leaves); fabric; thread; pen

The Sweetest Thing

Megan Snyder
St. George, Utah

Supplies: Cardstock; patterned paper (Chatterbox); rub-on letters (American Crafts); letter stickers (SEI); tag (Stampin' Up); chipboard heart (Heidi Swapp); rub-on word (Target); brad; thread; pen

Handwritten journaling: For a Valentine's Day treat, Mommy bought heart cookies. Gotta love pink and red Valentine sugar cookies! Yummy!

we LOVE cookies!

Happy Valentine's 2007

We Love Cookies!

Michelle St. Clair
Fuquay Varina, North Carolina

Supplies: Patterned paper (Doodlebug); scalloped cardstock (Bazzill); brads, photo turns (Queen & Co.); rub-on letters (American Crafts); rub-on word (Making Memories); pen; letter stickers (Doodlebug, EK Success)

tastes good

3 bananas for breakfast

'= 6 MAR 2006

ONE HAPPY MONKEY!

Tastes Good

Greta Hammond
Elkhart, Indiana

Supplies: Cardstock; chipboard letters and shapes, patterned paper (Scenic Route); die-cut letters and shapes (Provo Craft); buttons (Autumn Leaves); rickrack; pen

3 Bananas

Sarah van Wijck
Avalon Beach, New South Wales, Australia

Supplies: Patterned paper (Creative Imaginations, Prima); chipboard letters, file folder (Heidi Swapp); letter stickers (Making Memories); stamps (7gypsies, Greener Pastures); ribbon (Chatterbox); pen

After training for 8 months,
3 times a week &
assisting for 40 hours in the
children's classes you
received your blue belt in
karate. Congratulations Babe!

THURSDAY
August 17, 2006

Great Scrapbook Idea!

It's no secret that color can convey a mood on your page, but it can also take a literal cue from your subject. With her husband moving from a green belt to a blue belt in karate, Crystal knew she had the perfect color scheme for her layout. Allow color to play an important part in your next design and you're likely to be pleased with the results.

Blue Belt

Crystal Jeffrey Rieger
Woodbridge, Ontario, Canada

Supplies: Cardstock; patterned paper (BasicGrey, KI Memories, Paper Company); letter stickers (Making Memories); rub-on letters (ChartPak, Heidi Swapp); journaling accent, transparent accents (Heidi Swapp); buttons; corner rounder; decorative scissors; floss; hole punch; pigment ink; ribbon (Michaels); stamp (Creative Imaginations); staples; thread; pen

Do You Tri

Michelle Coleman
Layton, Utah

Supplies: Digital papers, stamps and embellishments (Little Dreamer Designs)

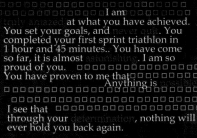

SWIM. BIKE. RUN.

DO YOU TRI
triathlon
06 24 06

You are such an inspiration.
I am truly amazed at what you have achieved. You set your goals, and never quit. You completed your first sprint triathlon in 1 hour and 45 minutes.. You have come so far, it is almost astonishing. I am so proud of you.
You have proven to me that Anything is possible.
I see that through your determination, nothing will ever hold you back again.

Celebrando Contigo

Maria Gallardo-Williams
Cary, North Carolina

Supplies: Cardstock; patterned paper (BasicGrey, Fancy Pants); letter stickers (American Crafts); ribbon, rub-on accents (Fancy Pants); staples

No Bikes

Champagne Severine
Dolomieu, France

Supplies: Digital cardstock (unknown); patterned paper (Simply Clean Digi Scraps); letters (Digital Design Essentials); round accents (Shabby Princess); stock photos (Stock Xchng); image editing software (Adobe)

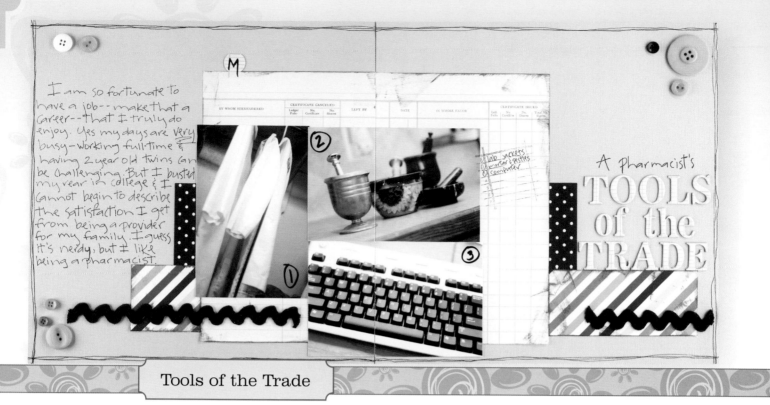

I am so fortunate to have a job--make that a Career--that I truly do enjoy. Yes my days are very busy-working full-time & having 2 year old twins can be challenging. But I busted my rear in college & I cannot begin to describe the satisfaction I get from being a provider for my family. I guess it's nerdy, but I like being a pharmacist.

A Pharmacist's TOOLS of the TRADE

Tools of the Trade

Melanie McFarlin
Lewisville, Texas

Supplies: Cardstock; patterned paper (Making Memories, Scenic Route); chipboard letters (Heidi Swapp); buttons (Autumn Leaves); stamp (October Afternoon); stamping ink; pen

Great Scrapbook Idea!

You may be sick of looking at them, but the tools that make your work possible are integral to your story. Photograph your tools and include them on a layout about how you spend your days—odds are, in a few years your days may be spent differently. And this is just the kind of thing that will fascinate future generations!

Equipped

Francine Clouden
Lyon, France

Supplies: Cardstock; patterned paper (Cosmo Cricket); chipboard letters (Heidi Swapp); chipboard accents (Fancy Pants, K&Co.); journaling sticker (Melissa Frances); distress ink; pen

Great Scrapbook Idea!

Lisa's layout is a great reminder to include photos of yourself on your pages. Hand the camera over to friends, relatives or even children to make sure your face is captured too. Then find a way to incorporate these rare images of yourself into a layout. Your family needs to remember you as more than just the person behind the camera!

Mom

Lisa Tutman-Oglesby
Mundelein, Illinois

Supplies: Patterned paper (Crate Paper); letter plates (Making Memories); ribbon (American Crafts); stamps (Creative Imaginations, Heidi Swapp, Stampendous); stamping ink; frame (Chatterbox); definition stickers (Jo-Ann's); flowers (K&Co.); circle punch; thread; pen

Parenting 101

Rachel Greig
Glenning Valley,
New South Wales, Australia

Supplies: Cardstock; patterned paper (Stamp-It Australia); rub-on letters (Imagination Project); letter stickers, tags (Making Memories); brads; flower stamp (Hero Arts); photo corners (Heidi Swapp); pen

Days Like This

Janine Wahl
Sylvan Lake, Alberta, Canada

Supplies: Cardstock; patterned paper (A2Z, Imagination Project, Polar Bear Press); letter stickers (American Crafts); acrylic letters (Making Memories); frames (Chatterbox); stamps (Heidi Swapp); solvent ink; pigment ink; glossy topcoat (Ranger); acrylic paint; brads, floral sequins, photo anchors (Queen & Co.); wire; pen

Great Scrapbook Idea!

Everywhere you look there are trinkets and tidbits that could easily find their way onto your next layout. As Jennifer demonstrates with her use of bobby pins and beads, using found objects on pages is not only inexpensive, but is also a great way to preserve a piece of daily life. Look around your house for tiny treasures that would nicely accent your next page.

Mom Style

Jennifer Armentrout
Lynchburg, Virginia

Supplies: Cardstock; patterned paper (BasicGrey); chipboard letters, journaling rub-ons (Heidi Swapp); rub-on letters (Making Memories); rub-on accents (7gypsies); stamps (Sassafras Lass); stamping ink; fabric tab (EK Success); beads; bobby pins; craft wire; pen

just so you know and so that i will never forget

just so you know that your smile gets you out of more trouble than i will ever admit

Just So You Know

Sara Dickey
Richmond, Virginia

Supplies: Patterned paper (My Mind's Eye); scalloped cardstock (Bazzill), rub-on letters (Daisy D's); brads

Circles

Jennifer Armentrout
Lynchburg, Virginia

Supplies: Cardstock; patterned paper (Sandylion); rub-on letters (Making Memories); rub-on accents (7gypsies, CherryArte); number stamps (Making Memories); stamping ink; pen

TODAY you ran

circles AROUND ME*

0 2 3 4 5 6 7 8 9 0
170

*literally.
I counted. too hot to be outside + pent-up energy = laps. rosy cheeks. smiles.*

✳ MAY CAUSE DROWSINESS

What It's All About

Maria Burke
Steinbach, Manitoba, Canada

Supplies: Cardstock; patterned paper (KI Memories, SEI); buttons, letter stickers, sticker accent (SEI); rub-on stitching (Die Cuts With A View); date stamp (Office Depot); circle punch; floss; pen

what its all about

being together - laughing & loving, having fun, no matter what's going on around us all the little day to day stuff that makes our lives so full of happiness just being together!

JUN 1 8 2006

An Average Work Day

Crystal Jeffrey Rieger
Woodbridge, Ontario, Canada

Supplies: Digital paper (Oscraps); letter and accent brushes, frame (ScrapArtist)

Jody Wilkinson
Bemidji, Minnesota

*Supplies: Cardstock; patterned paper, plastic
flowers (American Crafts); brads; acrylic
paint; paper glaze (Duncan)*

Deciding to go back to
work was just as dif-
ficult as deciding to
stay home. Am I doing
the right thing? Will
they be OK at daycare?
Are they having fun?
Adjusting? Are the
other kids being nice
to them? Are they
being nice to other
kids? Some days I hate
to admit it but I am
glad to be able to
drop them off and go
to work. I enjoy my
job. I like being able
to spend time with my
coworkers and I love
learning new things.
It s nice to have that
little bit of freedom.
Other days I miss them
so much and I want
them with me. Also,
coming home to a very
messy house and trying
to get supper together
with a toddler and a 3
year old clamoring for
my attention makes me
wonder if it is worth
it.

TORN

It is difficult to
balance it all some
days but I think this
is going to be OK.
This world is not a
perfect place and we
have to do what it
takes. So often I am
torn about leaving
them at daycare and
going on to work but
they are good girls,
growing up strong and
most importantly they
know I love them no
matter where I am.

Great Scrapbook Idea!

If you're looking for a way to use your
leftover letter stickers and rub-ons,
why not take a cue from Gretchen's
layout? Utilizing different stickers, rub-
ons, chipboard and journaling strips,
Gretchen was able to make a statement
with her journaling. Mix and match your
leftovers for a funky look that makes
you trendy and frugal at the same time!

When

Gretchen McElveen
Helena, Alabama

*Supplies: Patterned paper (Junkitz, My Mind's Eye); letter
stickers (BasicGrey, Heidi Swapp, Making Memories);
chipboard accent, rub-on letters (Heidi Swapp);
chipboard letters (Junkitz); dimensional adhesive; pen*

For Me

Courtney Walsh
Winnebago, Illinois

Supplies: Patterned paper; brads, chipboard letters, photo turns, ribbon holders (Queen & Co.)

I needed to look at this picture today. I needed to do something with it. I needed it... for me. See, it's not been a good few days for me. I'm not sure what's going on, but being cooped up with the snow - and you, missing so much school because you've been sick... it's just completely messed up our schedule, and when you get bored, you get hard. And you've been really, really hard. I have to admit, today, I'm feeling the pressure. My nerves are shot. I'm just trying to breathe... a lot. So, I took out this picture because it's one of my favorites. And it's of you. Sweet, adorable you. Smart and funny just like always... and somehow it makes me feel better... and somehow I'm refocused on what's important... and somehow doing this for me is suddenly okay. So this one, it's just for me.

Great Scrapbook Idea!

You might not be able to print in white ink, but you can certainly fake the look with a word processing program. Simply open a text box, fill with your desired color and then select white as your text color. Print the entire block as Tonya's done here with both the brown journaling blocks and the large blue rectangle behind her photo. Once you've learned this versatile trick, printing in white is easy!

Secrets Uncovered

Tonya Joy Kent
Anchorage, Alaska

Supplies: Cardstock; patterned paper (Chatterbox); correction tape runner (Paper Mate); transparent flowers (Heidi Swapp); brads (Making Memories); stamping ink; thread

I have shown all my underclothing to a group of Uruguayans while I tumbled down the stairs in a dress.

I once burned a postcard from another girl before it ever got into the hands of my ex-boyfriend

I have mastered the art of peeking at and re-wrapping Christmas gifts.

Michael Jackson posters with "Vote for Tonya or Beat It!" was my unsuccessful campaign for the 5th grade elections.

I once ran straight into a steel pole while attempting a brave getaway from TP'ing my crush.

secrets uncovered

Nov '06

The Gift

Hillary Heidelberg
New York, New York

Supplies: Cardstock; patterned paper (American Crafts); rub-on swirl (BasicGrey); rub-on stitches (Autumn Leaves); corner rounder; hole punch; pen; Haettenschweiler title font (Microsoft)

The Gift.

Our wedding date was set for 9/15/2001. I was nervous but very excited. On 9/11/2005, the unthinkable happened. And everything changed. But you were determined that our love, and our impending commitment would not be lost in the tragedy. And so it was, on 9/12/2001, you managed to travel from uptown Manhattan, past Ground Zero, all the way to Brooklyn. You made it all the way to the store where we had picked out Indian-inspired wedding rings just one year earlier. And on this day, you bought me a gorgeous ruby necklace as a wedding gift. You did this all to show me just how much I mean to you. And everytime I wear it, I am reminded of your love for me. I am reminded of the kind of person you are, the kind of person who values going the distance for the one he loves. The kind of person who lets *nothing* get in the way of demonstrating his love. The kind of person who truly believes in love in action. The kind of person I was lucky enough to marry.

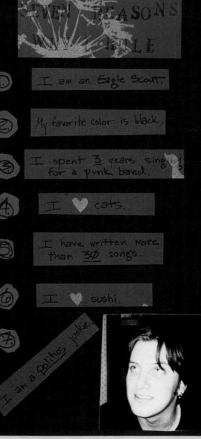

SEVEN REASONS WHY TITLE

1. I am an Eagle Scout.
2. My favorite color is black.
3. I spent 3 years singing for a punk band.
4. I ♥ cats.
5. I have written more than 30 songs.
6. I ♥ sushi.
7. I am a politics junkie.

Seven Reasons

Matt Wagner
Cincinnati, Ohio

Supplies: Cardstock; patterned paper (Hambly, Rouge de Garance); letter stamps (Hero Arts); pen

I Love You Every Day

Collette Osuna
Eastpointe, Michigan

Supplies: Cardstock; letter stickers, patterned paper, transparent accents (Heidi Grace); brads; corner rounder

In the hustle and bustle of hurried life,
it's not hard to forget to take the time
to appreciate all that I am thankful for.
There are so many people I love,
So many places that bring me joy
and the things?
They are just extras.

Chill

Lisa Botte
North Billerica, Massachusetts

Supplies: Cardstock; patterned paper (BasicGrey, KI Memories); rub-on letters, small brads (Making Memories); letter stickers (American Crafts); chipboard brackets, heart accent, large flower (Heidi Swapp); large brad, small flowers (Bazzill); distress ink; ribbon (American Crafts, Jo-Ann's, Making Memories, Michaels, Morex); eyelets; pen

Great Scrapbook Idea!

Not every layout has to be about a memory   some pages act as important reminders just for you. Gretchen's layout is a great example of how to pull a favorite quotation onto a page to keep it at the forefront of your mind. When you've got something significant to tell yourself, make it permanent by putting it on a layout. Even if no one else ever sees it, the reminder is more than worth the effort.

Remember

Gretchen McElveen
Helena, Alabama

Supplies: Patterned paper (BasicGrey, Cosmo Cricket, Scenic Route, Scrapworks); patterned transparency (My Mind's Eye); stamps (FontWerks, Heidi Swapp); fabric flower (Junkitz); journaling accent (Heidi Swapp); staples; dimensional adhesive; pen

It's My Life

Kim Christensen
Fair Oaks, California

Supplies: Digital flowers, letters, paint strokes, paper, tags (ScrapArtist); paper tear (Digital Paper Tearing); digital silk flowers (CD Muckosky); cardboard flowers (Misty Cato); Adler, DynoLabel, Susie's Hand fonts (Internet download)

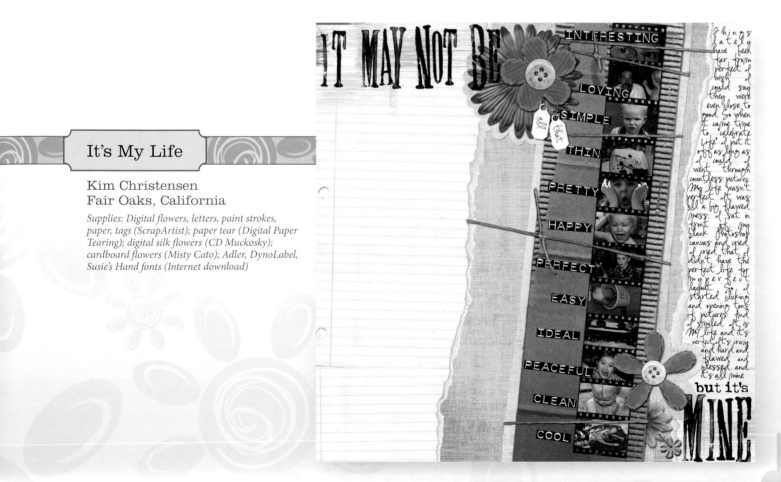

Fear of Heights

Maria Burke
Steinbach, Manitoba, Canada

Supplies: Cardstock; patterned paper (Creative Imaginations, SEI); letter stickers (BasicGrey); epoxy stickers (SEI); rub-on accent (Making Memories); corner rounder; pen

Summer '06

I've always had a fear of heights

I just don't like that feeling of being up high

Every now and then, I suck it up and

go down the slide at the park

FeaR OF HeiGHTS

Seems harmless enough, right?
So why is it every time I see one I cringe? Well, because if I see it, that means you see it and one of two things will surely follow.

1. You will insist on turning it on and if I deny you, it will initiate a full-blown tantrum with screams so loud the entire neighborhood will hear. OR

2. I will turn it on and you will play happily for four hours, at which point I will turn it off and the above tantrum will take place anyway.

Who would have thought the common garden hose could cause such turmoil in the life of a 2 year old and his mother?

the common
gardenhose

sheesh!

The Common Garden Hose

Deena Wuest
Goessel, Kansas

Supplies: Digital elements (Designer Digitals); image editing software (Adobe); Avant Garde, Broken 15 fonts (Internet download)

A New Perspective

Sandra Stanton
Northfield, New Jersey

Supplies: Digital page kit (ScrapDish); brushes, duct tape accent (Digi Chick); shadow actions (Traci Murphy); folded corner action (Scrapbook Graphics), Diesel, Dirty Ego, Peu Jenny Script fonts (Internet download)

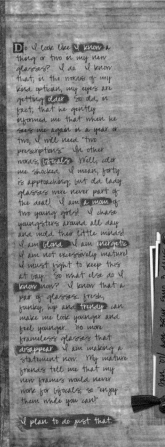

My Journey

Nicole Martel
Crownsville, Maryland

Supplies: Patterned paper (Imaginisce, We R Memory Keepers); word tags (My Mind's Eye); brads; sticker accents (Chatterbox); leaves (Prima); transparency

I Am...

Ariadna Wiczling
Kartuzy, Pomorskie, Poland

Supplies: Digital elements (Digi Shoppe, Scrap Girls); Depot, Depressionist Three, Maszyna Aeg, Rock It fonts (Internet download)

I Wanna Talk About Me

Mou Saha
Tampa, Florida

Supplies: Patterned paper (Making Memories, Prima); chipboard and plastic accents (American Crafts); frame (Making Memories); acrylic paint; stamping ink; brad (Pebbles); crocheted flower (Michaels); image editing software (Adobe); Ashley, Bloktype, BlueNorma, Cheltpress Trial fonts (Internet download)

Flower Child

Rachel Greig
Glenning Valley, New South Wales,
Australia

*Supplies: Cardstock; patterned paper (Sassafras Lass); letter
stickers (Making Memories); ribbon (May Arts); dye ink;
tags (Avery); corner rounder; pen*

1974 - the year when a postage stamp cost 7¢. A litre of milk cost 26¢ and when colour TV was trialed the show Happy Days hit the screens with The Fonz! Whitlam was our prime minister, and Darwin was hit by Cyclone Tracey. The year my grandparents moved to a new farm "Wirraway". Flared pants & paisley prints were all in fashion. And it was the year I was born.

Rachel Anneka. Born 1974 during the flower child era. Photo taken on my 32nd birthday 2006

England 1976

Mary Anne Humes
Cheney, Washington

*Supplies: Patterned paper, letter stickers
(BasicGrey); circle cutter; thread; pen*

Great Scrapbook Idea!

Try this technique to draw attention to portions of your photographs: Using image editing software, create a duplicate layer of your photo and convert it to black and white. Then use the eraser tool to allow the color to show through in the areas you want highlighted. This is an easy way to get striking results!

Just Add Spice

Mou Saha
Tampa, Florida

Supplies: Cardstock; patterned paper (Daisy D's, Making Memories); brads, clips, foam stamps, glitter, letter stickers (Making Memories); image editing software (Adobe); acrylic paint; date stamp (Signet); stamping ink; crocheted flower, lace; tags, yarn (unknown); thread; pen

Hopeful

Deborah Simon
Carmel, Indiana

Supplies: Cardstock; patterned paper (KI Memories, Reminisce, SEI); stamps (Making Memories); stamping ink; ribbon (BasicGrey, unknown); brads, buttons, gel stickers (SEI); thread

This is Me

Gretchen McElveen
Helena, Alabama

Supplies: Cardstock; chipboard letter, fabric ruler, patterned paper, ribbon (Junkitz); acrylic paint; staples; pen

Looking Back Yet Looking Ahead

Laura Achilles
Littleton, Colorado

Supplies: Patterned paper (Scenic Route); chipboard letters (Heidi Swapp, Scenic Route); ribbon (Offray); paper clip; acrylic paint; transparency

the signature of god is written in flowers

Amy Cutler
Irvona, Pennsylvania

Supplies: Patterned paper (Cosmo Cricket, Dream Street); patterned transparency (Hambly); chipboard bookplate, letter stickers (Heidi Swapp); die-cut letters (My Mind's Eye); stamps (ScrapTrends); pigment ink

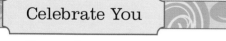

Celebrate You

Peggy Severins
Raamsdonksveer, Noord-Brabant,
The Netherlands

Supplies: Cardstock; die-cut squares, patterned paper (Urban Lily); die-cut stars (Sizzix); die-cut circles (Provo Craft); paper piercer; staples

You Remind Me

Amy Peterman
Muskegon, Michigan

Supplies: Cardstock; patterned paper (Autumn Leaves, KI Memories, Scrapworks); chipboard flower, patterned transparency (KI Memories); rub-on accents (My Mind's Eye); acrylic paint; staples; pen

Great Scrapbook Idea!

Love the look of transparent letters like those in Amy's layout? You can achieve this look simply by using a word processing program. Type your text into a new document, change the font to an outline style, and print it on a transparency. Then cut around the outline and add paint to the edges of your letters to make them stand out. Easy, hand-made transparent embellishments!

Hope Blooms

Andrea Wiebe
Westbank, British Columbia, Canada

Supplies: Cardstock; patterned paper (Fontwerks); letter stickers (Sandylion); decorative punch (Marvy); buttons; floss; notepaper; stamping ink; pen

Embrace Life

Michelle Van Etten
Riverview, Florida

Supplies: Cardstock; chipboard accents, patterned paper (Scenic Route); chipboard letters (Heidi Swapp); twill; chalk ink; adhesive foam; corner rounder

"Life is not about how many breathes you take, but about the moments that take your breathe away."

James I am reminded of this quote every time I see you and your daddy at the beach. We take you to the beach weekly and you and your dad play for hours. You have such a magical relationship. I am glad I was able to capture this embrace. These pictures were taken at NAS Beach in Pensacola Florida August 19th 2006.

WHEREEVER YOU GO...

NO MATTER WHAT THE WEATHER

ALWAYS BRING YOUR OWN

S U N S H I N E

Sunshine

Tish Treadaway
Harrisburg, North Carolina

Supplies: Cardstock; flower, letter stickers, patterned paper, quote stickers (Bo-Bunny); button; ribbon (unknown); thread

Great Scrapbook Idea!

If you've got scrap paper lying around, you can easily create a stunning layout. Try clustering lots of shapes closely together to create a unique design. This look could easily be created using any shaped punch, and by placing the punches in close proximity to each other. You'll end up with a high-impact design to liven up any layout!

If the sight of the blue skies fills you with joy,

if a blade of grass springing up in the fields has the power to move you,

if the simple things of nature have a message that you understand—

rejoice

for your soul is alive...

Rejoice

Sandi Minchuk
Merrillville, Indiana

Supplies: Cardstock; chipboard letters, patterned paper (Scenic Route); distress ink; thread; pen

the Circle game

Kerry, when I see this old picture of you,
I think of a favorite song of mine...

...and the seasons they go round and round
And the painted ponies go up and down
We're captive on the carousel of time.
We can't return, we can only look behind
From where we came
And go round and round and round
In the circle game...

– Joni Mitchell

The Circle Game

Sara Bohl
Mason City, Iowa

Supplies: Cardstock; patterned paper, ribbon, rickrack (BasicGrey); chipboard letters (Heidi Swapp, Making Memories, Pressed Petals); rub-on letters (Deja Views); flower, mirror accent (Hobby Lobby); acrylic paint; pigment ink; decorative scissors

There are so many possibilities just waiting to be explored......

POSSIBILITIES

April 2006

Great Scrapbook Idea!

Make a statement by enlarging your photo to reach the edges of your layout as Deena has done here. You may even consider printing a photo to the size of your layout and using it as the page's background. Once the photo is printed, embellish directly on it for a unique, larger-than-life look.

Possibilities

Deena Wuest
Goessel, Kansas

Supplies: Digital elements (Designer Digitals); image editing software (Adobe); Steelfish font (Internet download)

Make a Wish

Marie Lottermoser
Bellevue, Washington

Supplies: Patterned paper (BasicGrey, Me & My Big Ideas); embossing powder; rhinestones; ribbon (EK Success); dimensional paint; pigment ink; pen

MAKE A WISH

I am so happy you both have such wonderful imaginations you can turn any day into fairy tale adventures.

BeLiEvE

Fun Time, Be Yourself

Charlene Teo
West Zone, Singapore

Supplies: Patterned paper (American Crafts, BasicGrey, Scenic Route); letter stickers (American Crafts, EK Success); die-cut card (My Mind's Eye); rub-on accents (Urban Lily); stamps (Cavallini, Impress Rubber Stamps, Purple Onion); flower (Prima)

A Wish

Kim Christensen
Fair Oaks, California

Supplies: Digital paper, letters (ScrapArtist); paper tear (Digital Paper Tearing); Susie's Hand font (Internet download)

chapter

HARD *to* FORGET

Life is made up of moments, and so are most of our memories.
From the simple seasonal recollections to the holidays we look
forward to with every passing year, certain aspects of our lives
are hard to forget. Instead of allowing your traditions to pass
you by unnoted, give yourself a moment or two to evaluate
the passage of time. What are the memories you want to hold
onto? You might convince yourself you'll never forget these
precious days, but odds are, in time, you will. So do yourself
a favor and scrapbook them while they are fresh and alive
in your mind. The following chapter is full of a variety of
creative ideas to scrapbook the unforgettable events that
make your life unforgettable.

Eat Cake

Shannon Brouwer
Gilbert, Arizona

Supplies: Cardstock; die-cut letters, number sticker, patterned paper (BasicGrey); chipboard letters (Heidi Swapp); brads; flower charm (Li'l Davis); chalk ink; chipboard accent (Imagination Project); ribbon (Offray); 2Peas Quirky font (Two Peas in a Bucket)

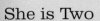

Great Scrapbook Idea!

Can't find the perfect frame for your photo? Create your own easily in a word processing program. Flanking the sides of your picture with a repeated sentiment will guarantee your focal point photo will be your focal point! Dress up the frame with a few small embellishments and admire the results!

She is Two

Katrina Huerta
Glendale, Arizona

Supplies: Cardstock; patterned paper (Dream Street); chipboard letters, photo corners, rhinestone circle (Heidi Swapp); letter stickers, paper frills (Doodlebug); stamp (FontWerks); rub-on accents (BasicGrey); pigment ink; pen

A Birthday to Remember

Brooke Bartimioli
Hayden, Idaho

Supplies: Cardstock; patterned paper (7gypsies, BasicGrey, K&Co., My Mind's Eye); stamps (Making Memories); brads; scrapper's floss (Karen Foster); label (Dymo); number chip (Li'l Davis); stamping ink; metal accents (unknown); pen

Mom & Doni were turning **50** on July 11th, 2006. A big bash was in the making, but things don't always go as planned. Mom would be spending her birthday in the hospital with Matt. She didn't mind at all; in situations like these, the **greatest gifts of family and wellness** are realized. Aaron and I decided to **surprise** her by meeting in Davis and heading up to Redding together (also with friend, Geoff Krieger). The eve before her birthday, Aaron walks into Matt's hospital room, **unannounced**. Mom cried, declaring what a great present his visit was. Ten minutes later, I walked into the room. Mom was shocked, and of course she cried again. Twenty-five minutes later, Geoff walked in, and we all had a good laugh. The next day, Mom's birthday, **Matt was released from the hospital!** We had a little party at Mom & Dad's with Doni, Bruce, Josh and Joe. I don't think Mom will ever forget her 50th birthday, spent with her **three kids**.

Make a Wish

Sandra Stanton
Northfield, New Jersey

Supplies: Digital page kit (Digi Chick); flower and tape measure elements, ribbon (Lily Pad); shadow actions (Traci Murphy); Madfont, Pea Shirley fonts (Internet download)

You Now

Lisa Carroll
Asheville, North Carolina

Supplies: Cardstock; patterned paper (BasicGrey, Scenic Route); letter stickers (Making Memories); chalk ink; brads (Provo Craft); staples

Great Scrapbook Idea!

As the birthday party planner, odds are getting the perfect birthday photos might not be the easiest task. Eliminate the pressure by taking a couple of portrait style shots of the birthday child and a few key details and then put the camera down to enjoy the party! You'll have photos to tell the story without the pressure of being behind a camera the whole time.

Lucky Number Seven

Michelle Coleman
Layton, Utah

Supplies: Digital papers, stamps and embellishments (Little Dreamer Designs)

Could swim the length of a 25-yard lap pool at the Rec. Ctr.

Could reach kitchen faucet without a step-stool

Started kindergarten

Learn to read & realize you love it

Learn to ride a bike without training wheels

Painted your bedroom in Bronco Orange & Blue

Skied for the first time (and many more)

Went to your first Rockies (MLB) Game

Decided NFL Football was your life

FEB for FEB
2006 2007

Great Scrapbook Idea!

Children change so quickly, it's likely that you won't remember what they loved at what age unless you write it down. Create pages to highlight your child's year just before he turns another year older with a simple list of the things he loves and what his year entailed. You'll love the comprehensive look back as you accumulate more pages each year!

While You Were Five

Carolyn A. Lontin
Highlands Ranch, Colorado

Supplies: Cardstock; patterned paper (My Mind's Eye); chipboard letters (BasicGrey, Maya Road); letter stickers (Arctic Frog); die-cut shapes (Provo Craft, My Mind's Eye, QuicKutz); arrow, journaling accent, clock accent (Heidi Swapp); rub-ons (7gypsies); brads, date stamp (Making Memories); sequin; ribbon (Strano); distress ink

Birthday Checklist

Summer Ford
Bulverde, Texas

Supplies: Cardstock; patterned paper (BasicGrey); letter stamps (Stampin' Up); date stamps; stamping ink; hole tabs (office supply store); chipboard number (Rusty Pickle); rhinestones (Jo-Ann's); ribbon (Offray); acrylic paint; sandpaper; corner rounder

Nickelodeon Valentine's Day cards. He also addressed a special card just for his bestest friend and brother, Andrew.

'07

This was the first year that he did it all by himself. Nathan decided which card to send to each friend, addressed them, put stickers on them, and folded up all 31 of his

Valentine Cards

Michelle St. Clair
Fuquay Varina, North Carolina

Supplies: Die-cut shapes, patterned paper (Sassafras Lass); chipboard letters (Imagination Project); rub-on letters (Making Memories); paper frills (Doodlebug)

Sharing the Love

Heather Dewaelsche
Fishers, Indiana

Supplies: Cardstock; patterned paper (Doodlebug, KI Memories); vellum; pigment ink; striped ribbon (American Crafts); ribbon, rickrack (unknown); valentine cards; Ballpark title font (Internet download)

Great Scrapbook Idea!

Kids love to keep valentines from their school friends. What better way to do that than with a pocket page to house them all in one place? Use festive hearts in coordinating patterned papers to create the perfect place for the tiny valentines your child brings home from school.

It didn't take long for Sarina to spot her first egg and within minutes she had more than she could carry.

Missy Neal
Campbell, California

Supplies: Cardstock; patterned paper (BasicGrey); chipboard letters (Pressed Petals, Scenic Route); chipboard accents (Pressed Petals, Trace Industries); stamps (Li'l Davis, Technique Tuesday); rub-on (unknown); pen

Great Scrapbook Idea!

We're all looking for ways to save time in our scrapbooking. Here's one: An easy way to add several photos to a layout is to line them up in an image editing software program and print them as one long strip. Instead of trimming them individually, you can space them prior to printing and cut them all at the same time.

Add Color

Charity Hassel
Jacksonville, Florida

Supplies: Cardstock; patterned paper (AdornIt); letter stickers (Arctic Frog); ribbon (SEI); paper frill (Doodlebug); mini brads (Queen & Co.); corner rounder; pen

add color

It took Alexander some time to get into coloring the Easter Eggs. Before long he had the eggs (and hands) colored! Having fun is as simple as adding color! Easter 2006

Great Scrapbook Idea!

Who says your journaling has to be in a straight line? If you're looking for a fun way to add journaling to your design, give this idea a try: Print your journaling and trim each word into its own strip of paper, then sew it down along a shape on your layout. You can save a little space and add journaling to any design just by thinking outside the box.

Easter Exhaustion

Melissa Kelley
Pueblo, Colorado

Supplies: Cardstock; sticker borders (Stemma); fabric photo corners, number stickers (Making Memories); rub-on letters (Autumn Leaves); thread

The Colors of Easter

Pam Callaghan
Bowling Green, Ohio

Supplies: Cardstock; patterned paper, tabs, transparency (Die Cuts With A View); rub-on accents (BasicGrey); ribbon (Making Memories); corner rounder

1stEGGhUnT

despite all plans for a perfect day, easter sunday began with a downpour — and with 9 two & three year-olds @ our home, we were in luck when the rain let up long enough for us to have our first egghunt. It was bank's 1st egghunt ever!

Great Scrapbook Idea!

Just looking around your scrap space you can find many new uses for different tools. For instance, you can create a whimsical dotted border on your layouts by using a little paint and the end of a paintbrush. Why not experiment with other tools to discover cool textures and unique looks.

1st Egg Hunt

April Foster
Bowling Green, Kentucky

Supplies: Cardstock; patterned paper (Making Memories); chipboard letters, rhinestone, tape (Heidi Swapp); letter stickers (Arctic Frog); acrylic paint; pen

Go Find Your Eggs

Wendy Inman
Virginia Beach, Virginia

Supplies: Cardstock; patterned paper, rub-on letters and accents, sticker accents (Karen Foster)

LOOK WHAT I FOUND

Hoppin' around

With those four words you eagerly ran toward the park area, into your very first neighborhood egg hunt. We had such a great time! I really enjoyed watching you unsuccessfully try to pick up two eggs at a time over and over. You were just too cute!

"go find your eggs!"

Breeze

Tina Albertson
Harlan, Indiana

Supplies: Patterned paper (SEI); scalloped cardstock (Bazzill); chipboard letters (Scenic Route); flowers (Mermaid Tears); ledger paper; sequins; pen

Garden of Delights

Melissa Kelley
Pueblo, Colorado

Supplies: Cardstock; patterned paper, ribbon, rub-on stems (Stemma); letter stamps (Making Memories); lace (Wrights); buttons (Autumn Leaves); dye ink, thread

Our Backyard Birds

Susan Hubbs
Orlando, Florida

Supplies: Cardstock; patterned paper (Urban Lily); rub-on letters (Imagination Project); chipboard letters (Heidi Swapp); flowers (Queen & Co.); brads; circle cutter; photo turns (Junkitz); thread

Picking Fruit

Brooke Bartimioli
Hayden, Idaho

Supplies: Cardstock; patterned paper (Stemma); rub-on accents (BasicGrey, Bo-Bunny); stamping ink; buttons, ribbon (unknown); pen

Great Scrapbook Idea!

Get up close and personal with the nature you find right in your own backyard. Not only is this a great way to get some photography practice with a subject you might not be used to photographing, but it's also a wonderful way to appreciate the beauty all around you!

Fleeting Friends

Amy Tara Koeppel
Hobe Sound, Florida

Supplies: Patterned paper, letter stickers, rickrack (BasicGrey); rub-on accents (Autumn Leaves, BasicGrey); distress ink; foam spacers; brads (Karen Foster); pen

Sweet Flowers

Liz Goldhawk
Lundon, Ontario, Canada

*Supplies. Digital elements (Shabby Princess);
AL Uncle Charles, Emmascript MVB, Favorite
Things fonts (Internet download)*

Beautiful Details

Krista L. Austin
Chicago, Illinois

*Supplies: Cardstock; rub-on word (Scenic Route); round letters (Li'l Davis);
brads, flowers (Queen & Co.); ribbon (May Arts); rub-on accent (BasicGrey)*

A Piece of Cake

April Foster
Bowling Green, Kentucky

Supplies: Cardstock; patterned paper (Making Memories); chipboard letters, rhinestone (Heidi Swapp); stamp (FontWerks); stamping ink; pen

Flower Girls

Stephanie A. Helmke
Defiance, Ohio

Supplies: Cardstock; flowers, frame, patterned paper, word accents (My Mind's Eye); ribbon (Chatterbox); rub-on letters (Imagination Project); circle punch; dimensional adhesive; dye ink; pen

July 4 Traditions

Brooke Bartimioli
Hayden, Idaho

Supplies: Cardstock; patterned paper (Chatterbox, Daisy D's, Wube); letter stamps (Provo Craft); pigment ink; letter stickers (Bo-Bunny); rub-on word (Daisy D's); brad; paper clip; pen

Great Scrapbook Idea!

The next time you're looking for an easy way to spice up your embellishments, consider going metallic! With all kinds of shiny items out there—from metallic inks to silver paint to shiny embroidery floss—it's easy to find a way to make your page sparkle.

Sparkler Fun

Greta Hammond
Elkhart, Indiana

Supplies: Cardstock; chipboard letters and shapes, patterned paper, rub-on letters (Imagination Project); brads; pigment ink

Giggles

Amy Peterman
Muskegon, Michigan

Supplies: Patterned paper (Making Memories, My Mind's Eye); letter stickers (EK Success); chipboard letters, frame (Heidi Swapp); sticker accents (7gypsies); stamps (Making Memories); rub-on accents (Chatterbox); acrylic paint; staples; correction tape (Bic); pen

4th of July

Jill Jackson-Mills
Roswell, Georgia

Supplies: Cardstock; patterned paper (Reminisce); ribbon, transparency (unknown); staples

Great Scrapbook Idea!

For an interesting way to cram tons of photos onto your page, consider creating a photo collage in any shape and size. From circles to squares to stars, this is an easy and unique way to incorporate countless pictures on one layout while providing visual interest.

4th of July

Courtney Walsh
Winnebago, Illinois

Supplies: Cardstock; patterned paper (Chatterbox); chipboard letters (All My Memories); letter stickers (Doodlebug); number sticker (Mustard Moon); buttons (Autumn Leaves); ribbon (Making Memories, Michaels); pen

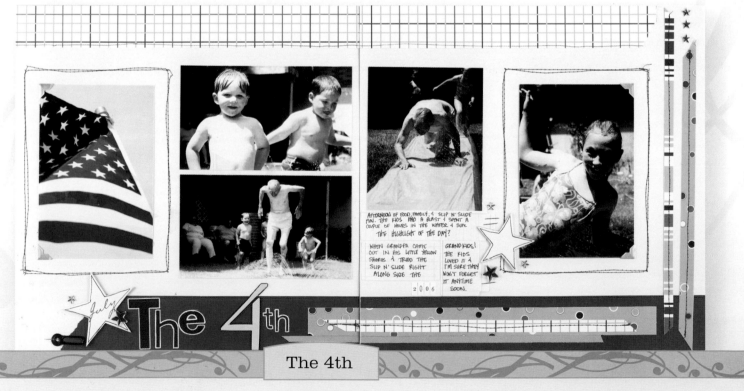

The 4th

Nicole Stark
Roy, Utah

Supplies: Cardstock; patterned paper (SEI); letter stickers (Arctic Frog, Three Bugs in a Rug); rub-on word (Die Cuts With A View); chipboard stars, journaling accent (Heidi Swapp); number stickers (Making Memories); photo turn (7gypsies); photo corners (3L); rhinestone stars (unknown); staples; thread; pen

The Best Part of Any Celebration is the Treats!

Suzy Plantamura
Laguna Niguel, California

Supplies: Cardstock; patterned paper (Daisy Bucket, unknown); chipboard letters (American Crafts); chipboard stars (Maya Road); stamping ink; pen

NYC Subway

Hillary Heidelberg
New York, New York

Supplies: Cardstock; patterned paper (CherryArte); rub-on letters (Making Memories); rub-on accent (7gypsies); sticker accents (Creative Imaginations, KI Memories); Blue Highway font (Internet download)

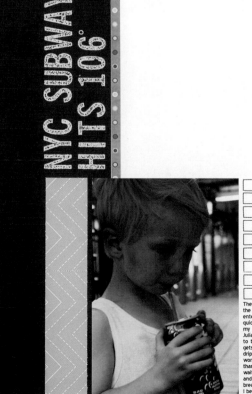

There are few things worse about city life than going down into the bowels of NYC subway system on a hot summer day. As we enter the subway, the full blast of hot, humid air hits us. We quickly hurry towards the turnstiles, and I say a quick prayer that my Metrocard still has another ride left on it. I swipe the card. Julian's stroller can't fit through the turnstile, so I frantically wave to the station agent to open the gate. As we near the tracks, it gets (unbelievably) warmer. I look around at the men and women dripping in their business suits and thank GOD that I no longer work in corporate America. Luca sips his cold Welch's soda that I thankfully remembered to get for him, and we wait. We wait and wait. We try not to move too much. Eventually the train comes, and as the ice cold air of the subway car hits us, everyone breathes a collective sigh of relief. Smiles break out, and Luca and I begin our ritual subway game of Guess the Animal.

Relax It's Summer!

Greta Hammond
Elkhart, Indiana

Supplies: Cardstock; scalloped cardstock (Bazzill); chipboard accents, patterned paper, rub-on letters (Imagination Project); chipboard letters (Heidi Swapp); rub-on accents (American Crafts); thread

Laugh Play Swim

Michelle Coleman
Layton, Utah

Supplies: Digital papers, stamps and embellishments (Little Dreamer Designs)

Katastrof

Tina Johansson
Sturefors, Östergötland, Sweden

Supplies: Cardstock; patterned paper (7gypsies, A2Z, Scenic Route); chipboard letters (Heidi Swapp); rub-on accent (BasicGrey); ribbon (unknown); button; acrylic paint; staple; corner rounder

A Day at the Park

Michelle Lanning
La Habra, California

Supplies: Cardstock; patterned paper, ribbon (American Crafts); chipboard letters (Heidi Swapp); flowers (Prima); journaling paper (Creative Imaginations); solvent ink; brads; staples; pen

Vroom

Tanisha Long
Roselle, New Jersey

*Supplies: Cardstock; patterned paper (Autumn
Leaves, MOD, Urban Lily); chipboard letters (Scenic
Route); chipboard swirl (Fancy Pants); buttons
(Autumn Leaves, SEI), rub-on accents (Autumn
Leaves, BasicGrey); dye ink; pen*

LOVE REMEMBER

my little man and
me just hanging at the
children's museum on the
day of courtney's birthday party
We had fun playing make believe Jan 2007

Museum of Nature & Science

Tracie Radtke
Chicago, Illinois

*Supplies: Digital kit (ScrapArtist); image editing software
(Adobe); LD Pretty font (Internet download)*

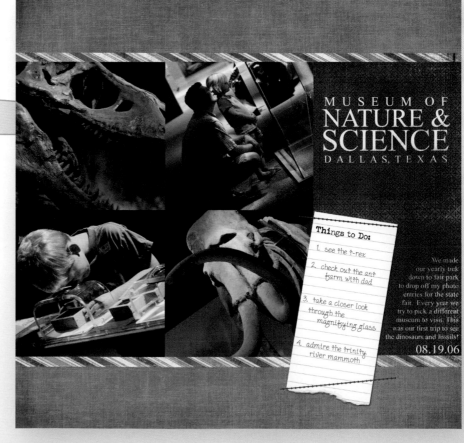

MUSEUM OF
NATURE &
SCIENCE
DALLAS, TEXAS

Things to Do:

1. see the t-rex

2. check out the ant
   farm with dad

3. take a closer look
   through the
   magnifying glass

4. admire the trinity
   river mammoth

We made
our yearly trek
down to fair park
to drop off my photo
entries for the state
fair. Every year we
try to pick a different
museum to visit. This
was our first trip to see
the dinosaurs and fossils!

08.19.06

Horse

Charity Hassel
Jacksonville, Florida

Supplies: Patterned paper, die-cut letters and shapes, tabs (Cosmo Cricket); pen

Seize the Day

Diane D. Michael
Mannington, West Virginia

Supplies: Digital page kit, papers and elements (Sweet Shoppe Designs)

Any time it rained this summer Emma would ask if we could go out & play in it. I would scan the skies for lightning & if we were free & clear we'd head out. At first Emma would scream & try to dodge between the drops but she'd soon succumb and dance in the rain.

rain dance

June 11, '06

Rain Dance

Keri Voigt
Evans, Colorado

Supplies: Cardstock; patterned paper (KI Memories); chipboard letters (Li'l Davis); acrylic paint; stamping ink; embossing powder; pen

Great Scrapbook Idea!

Look for new ways to make your patterns not only appealing to the eye, but functional as well. For example, let your blocked patterns pull double duty by dressing up your page while creating a frame for your tiniest photos.

Hangin' with the Jellies

Courtney Kelly
Anchorage, Alaska

Supplies: Cardstock; letter stickers, metal letter, patterned paper (American Crafts); foam adhesive; corner rounder

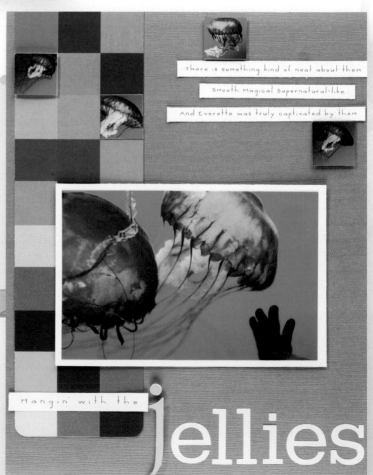

There is something kind of neat about them
Smooth magical supernatural-like
And Everette was truly captivated by them

Hangin' with the **jellies**

Summer Camp

Terri Hayes
Cary, North Carolina

Supplies: Cardstock; patterned paper (CherryArte, Paper Studio); letter stickers (Doodlebug); rub-on words (Chatterbox); sticker accents (Design Originals, Pebbles); rhinestone star (Me & My Big Ideas); felt arrows (American Crafts); brad (Queen & Co.); pen

Fresh

Hillary Heidelberg
New York, New York

Supplies: Digital cardstock, title letters (Sweet Shoppe Designs); patterned paper (Sugar Giggles); rub-on accent (unknown); Elementary SF font (Internet download)

fresh.

fresh blueberries while basking in the Florida sun. There's nothing like it.

Piece of Heaven

Greta Hammond
Elkhart, Indiana

Supplies: Cardstock; chipboard flowers and letters, patterned paper, rub-on letters (Imagination Project)

a Piece of HEAVEN

Watch Hill, Rhode Island has always had a soft spot in my heart. It is a magical place to me. A quaint little town right on the ocean where many wealthy families from the city have their "summer cottages". The town comes to life after school is let out and people swarm to soak up everything summer. The beaches are breathtaking, the New England architecture is pristine and the downtown shops are quaint. Every night you see the children line up for the one hundred year old Flying Horse Carousel, in hopes of catching the brass ring. And every night, people wait in line for ice cream at the ice cream shop. Watch Hill is a world of its own. A place where the worries of everyday are non-existent. A place that signifies what summer is all about. A place that makes you feel good every time you visit, a little piece of heaven.

Do You Believe in Magic?

Mou Saha
Tampa, Florida

Supplies: Cardstock; acrylic paint; Mickey Mouse tags (EK Success); pen

Goofy Girl

Kerry Zerff
Regina, Saskatchewan, Canada

Supplies: Cardstock; patterned paper (SEI), stamps (Gelatins); embossing powder; stamping ink; corner rounder; thread; pen

Great Scrapbook Idea!

Don't create happiness where there wasn't any. While a trip to the amusement park may be something you want to remember as nothing but fun, make sure to document the real story behind the photos, even if it's not the most pleasant. The result may be a truly sweet layout that captures your child's personality right at that moment.

Too Short

Laura Achilles
Littleton, Colorado

Supplies: Cardstock; patterned paper (Crate Paper); letter stickers (American Crafts); stamps (Autumn Leaves); stamping ink; decorative scissors; pen

Great Scrapbook Idea!

Can't find the space for titles or journaling? Write directly on your photos! You'll save time rearranging your layout as well as save space. Do it digitally and save even more time. Just add text to your photos using a photo editing software program and then print them out. What a fun, practical way to punch up your pictures!

Delight in Everything

Liana Suwandi
Wylie, Texas

Supplies: Cardstock; patterned paper (unknown); chipboard accents (Bazzill, Fancy Pants); flower (Bazzill); stamp (Stampin' Up); ribbon, rickrack (Fancy Pants); sticker (7gypsies, K&Co.); decorative tape (Making Memories); brad (SEI); rub-on accents (Creative Imaginations); acrylic paint; pen

Michigan Avenue Shopping

Greta Hammond
Elkhart, Indiana

Supplies: Cardstock; patterned paper (Fancy Pants); die-cut letters (Provo Craft); chipboard letters (Heidi Swapp); flower (Bazzill); button; rub-on accents (My Mind's Eye); digital frames (Two Peas in a Bucket)

Brussels

Diane D. Michael
Mannington, West Virginia

Supplies: Digital paper, brushes and elements (FishScraps)

The alleyways and small streets running off the Grand Place are filled with wonderful small shops of delightful goods. Belgium is famous for its chocolates, its lace, its pastries and candies, and its frites. We found them all off of Grand Place. I discovered Dandoy's and a love affair with Belgian pastries. Also, Brussels is a major European fashion center. 10/07.

SHOPPING

Memories of Coney Island

Andrea Amu
McClure, Pennsylvania

Supplies: Cardstock; patterned paper (BasicGrey); patterned transparency (My Mind's Eye); letter stickers (American Crafts, Me & My Big Ideas); sticker accents (Creative Imaginations, EK Success); stamps (Stampin' Up); stamping ink; fasteners (EK Success)

Air Show Fun

Kelly Bryan
Avon Lake, Ohio

Supplies: Cardstock; patterned paper (My Mind's Eye); letter stickers (Heidi Swapp); rub-on letters (American Crafts); rub-on numbers (7gypsies); rub-on accents (7gypsies, BasicGrey)

Great Scrapbook Idea!

One easy way to really make a photo stand out is to add a frame around it. Shirley's frame can be easily duplicated with any ribbon, buttons, even brads. Simply line the embellishments around the photos and watch them pop right off the page! This is a great way to use up scraps left on your table as well.

Summer Vacation

Shirley Chai
Ringwood, Victoria, Australia

Supplies: Patterned paper (My Mind's Eye); binder clips, bottle caps, wooden letters (Li'l Davis); letter stickers (BasicGrey); paper frills (Doodlebug); sticker accents (EK Success, Heidi Swapp); pen

Great Scrapbook Idea!

Not every part of every photo needs to remain visible on your layouts. Consider utilizing the empty space in your photo to showcase another smaller photo. This is an ideal way to incorporate more photos on your layout, but it also gives you some interesting design options as well.

The Best of Times

Beth Sears
Quispamsis, New Brunswick, Canada

Supplies: Cardstock; patterned paper (Chatterbox); rub-on letters and accents (Creative Imaginations); ribbon (Michaels); stamping ink; snaps (Making Memories); circle punch; decorative punch

The Best of Times are always the ones we share as a family. On this hot summer day we enjoyed the view from Cadillac Mountain. It's one of those moments that pass so quickly yet leave such a lasting memory.

Indiana State Fair

Heather Dewaelsche
Fishers, Indiana

Supplies: Cardstock; dimensional adhesive; GoldRush, LainieDaySH title fonts (Internet download)

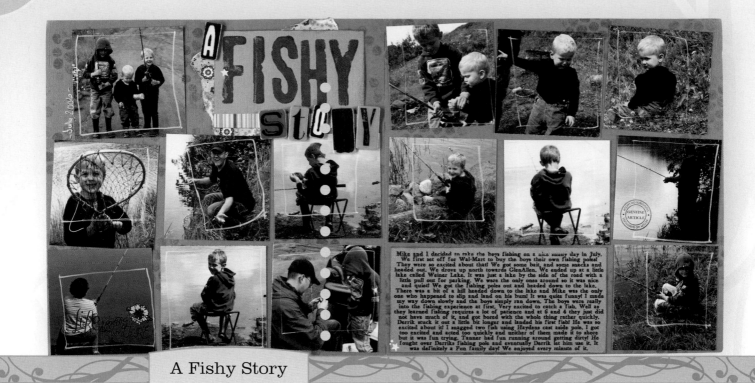

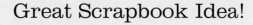

A Fishy Story

Sara Wise
Wasilla, Alaska

Supplies: Cardstock; patterned paper (Chatterbox); chipboard letters (Li'l Davis); stamps (Making Memories, Stampin' Up); acrylic paint; rub-on accents (Fancy Pants, MaisyMo); bubble wrap; pen

Great Scrapbook Idea!

The next time you want to throw the packaging from your latest delivery in the garbage, reconsider! Try using the bubble wrap as a stamp for your next scrapbook layout. While you're at it, experiment by adding paint to other objects around the house like paper towels, silk flowers, and sponges. What a fun way to create one-of-a-kind patterned papers and designs.

Treasure

Heather Verrier
Grimsby, Ontario, Canada

Supplies: Cardstock; patterned paper (Melissa Frances); chipboard letters (Scenic Route); label (Dymo); stamp (Gelatins); stamping ink; tabs (Making Memories); ribbon (unknown); beads (Lä Dé Dä)

Waterfront

Kerry Zerff
Regina, Saskatchewan, Canada

Supplies: Cardstock; patterned paper (Autumn Leaves, MOD); photo corners, rub-on letters (Heidi Swapp); rub-on accents (Autumn Leaves); pen

Summer Memories

Sarah van Wijck
Avalon Beach, New South Wales, Australia

Supplies: Cardstock; patterned paper (7gypsies); rub-on accent (BasicGrey); tag (Creative Imaginations); large brad (Bazzill); paper clip, ribbon, sequins (unknown); pen

Beach Boys

Erika Smith
Lorain, Ohio

Supplies: Patterned paper (Scenic Route); scalloped cardstock (Bazzill); plastic letters (KI Memories); chipboard letters (American Crafts); letter stickers (EK Success); rub-on accent (BasicGrey); sticker accents (7gypsies); decorative scissors; solvent ink; date stamp; thread

Great Scrapbook Idea!

With so many cute products out there, why should patterned paper get to have all the fun? Next time you want to dress up a background, turn to ribbons, buttons and rickrack! These embellishments are so versatile they shine as page backgrounds as well as accents. Go ahead and give it a try!

Delight

Yvette Adams
Banks, Australian Capital
Territory, Australia

Supplies: Cardstock; patterned paper (Urban Lily); rub-on letters (DecAdry); photo corners, rub-on words (Heidi Swapp); rub-on accent (BasicGrey); brads; buttons; ribbon; rickrack; staples; tag; thread

The Last Day of Vacation

Linda Sobolewski
Guilford, Connecticut

Supplies: Cardstock; chipboard letters, patterned paper (Scenic Route); letter stickers (Creative Imaginations); chipboard accents (Heidi Swapp); brads, flower (Queen & Co.); rub-on accents (7gypsies); vellum; thread

What Will He Remember?

Nic Howard
Pukekohe, South Aukland,
New Zealand

Supplies: Cardstock; patterned paper (Scenic Route); chipboard letters (Everlasting Keepsakes, Scenic Route); stamps (Little Black Dress); rub-on accents (7gypsies); solvent and watermark inks; beads; photo corners (Heidi Swapp); glass finish (Plaid); pen; Daniel Black, My Own Topher fonts (Internet download)

Sweet Hugs

Terri Hayes
Cary, North Carolina

Supplies: Cardstock; patterned paper (Reminisce); epoxy letters (Around the Block); rub-on word (My Mind's Eye); paper frills (Doodlebug); photo corner (American Crafts); button (Autumn Leaves); pen

Found It!

Holly Pittroff
Mooresville, North Carolina

Supplies: Cardstock; patterned paper (Anna Griffin); chipboard letters (Heidi Swapp); monogram tag (My Mind's Eye); waxed cord (Darice); spiral clip; stamping ink; transparency; pen

Great Scrapbook Idea!

To create the background on this layout, Holly printed enlarged photos from the pumpkin patch onto a transparency. This not only reinforced the theme of the layout but allowed her to incorporate another photo from her trip in a unique way. Change up your photo printing regimen and test out the transparency. You might end up hooked!

Autumn Hayride

Kristen Swain
Bear, Delaware

Supplies: Cardstock; letter stickers, patterned paper (Bo-Bunny); circle punch; buttons; pen

Fall

Kay Rogers
Midland, Michigan

Supplies: Cardstock; chipboard letters, patterned paper, sticker accents (KI Memories); ribbon (American Crafts); journaling stamp (Autumn Leaves); stamping ink; corner rounder; pen

Picking Apples

Greta Hammond
Elkhart, Indiana

Supplies: Cardstock; patterned paper (Scenic Route); chipboard letters (Pressed Petals); buttons, rub-on letters (Making Memories); felt; photo turn (Sizzix); brad; thread

Great Scrapbook Idea!

Doodles don't have to be flat! If you're looking for a way to perk up your doodling adventures, why not sew in metallic thread over your doodles? Not handy with a sewing machine? Try hand-stitching to add texture and dimension to your free form works of art!

Autumn Stroll

Janine Wahl
Sylvan Lake, Alberta, Canada

Supplies: Patterned paper (We R Memory Keepers); chipboard letters (Heidi Swapp, Li'l Davis); stamps (Technique Tuesday); embossing powder; beads; sequins; thread; pen; Poor Richard font (Internet download)

October Sky

Debbie Webster
Layton, Utah

Supplies: Cardstock; patterned paper (Paper Tapestry, Scenic Route); ribbon (unknown); brad; lamination sheets (Xyron); thread; leaves

One Fine Day

Francine Clouden
Lyon, France

Supplies: Cardstock; patterned paper, rub-on accents (Fancy Pants); letter stickers (American Crafts); stamps (Autumn Leaves, Hampton Art, Making Memories); metal rim tag (Making Memories); stamping ink; pen

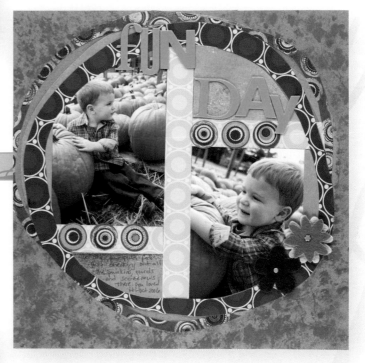

Fun Day

Charity Hassel
Jacksonville, Florida

Supplies: Kraft cardstock; patterned paper (BasicGrey, Dream Street); chipboard letters (Heidi Swapp); acrylic paint; flowers (American Crafts); brad; pen

Sweater Season

Rita Shimniok
Cross Plains, Wisconsin

Supplies: Patterned paper (Crafter's Workshop, Daisy D's); chipboard letters (Doodlebug, Heidi Swapp, Making Memories, Scenic Route, We R Memory Keepers); rub-on letters (Making Memories); flowers (Michaels); brads; fibers (EK Success, unknown); acrylic paint; pen

Just Wrong

Nicole Stark
Roy, Utah

Supplies: Cardstock; patterned paper (KI Memories, Scenic Route, Stemma); chipboard letters (Fancy Pants); patterned transparency, rub-on accent (Hambly); chipboard star (Li'l Davis); brads; label, tag (Avery); sticker accent (7gypsies); holiday tag (Making Memories); ribbon (Stemma); pigment ink; pen

Zoo Boo

Greta Hammond
Elkhart, Indiana

Supplies: Cardstock; chipboard letters, patterned paper (Scenic Route); sticker accents (Making Memories)

Great Scrapbook Idea!

If you're looking for a unique way to add a title to your page, think about going vertical! This opens up so many possibilities for your design, and gives you the chance to mix it up a little bit. With a title along the vertical side of a photo, the eye is even more drawn to the focal point.

Trick or Treat

Susan Weinroth
Centerville, Minnesota

Supplies: Cardstock; patterned paper (Heidi Grace); buttons, letter stickers (American Crafts); brads, photo turns (Queen & Co.); epoxy stickers (Cloud 9); decorative punches (Fiskars); adhesive foam; thread

Trick or Treat

Lisa Tutman-Oglesby
Mundelein, Illinois

Supplies: Cardstock; letter stickers, patterned paper (KI Memories); die-cut letters and flowers (QuicKutz); ribbon (American Crafts); brads (Hot Off The Press); word stickers (EK Success); acrylic paint; circle cutter; hole punch; thread; transparency

Pouty Pooh

Dawn Hagewood
Sterling, Virginia

Supplies: Cardstock; patterned paper (Heidi Grace); chipboard letters (Scenic Route); rub-on letters (American Crafts); slide mount (Loresch)

For the life of me I could not get you to smile at your school Halloween parade this year. You walked around with such a serious, pouty face. It was until later that night, when we were trick or treating, that you finally began to smile and have fun.

I so wanted a little girl. And then you finally came along and look what I did to you. No frilly princess dress, no cutsy ladybug or butterfly costume. No, for Halloween I bought black Chuck's, a skull t-shirt, and made a black tutu. Yes, you were a punk ballerina. Not so girly, but so very adorable!

Punk Ballerina

Michele Skinner
Burnsville, Minnesota

Supplies: Cardstock; patterned paper (BasicGrey); patterned transparency (Hambly); letter stickers (Making Memories, Three Bugs in a Rug); chipboard letters (K&Co.); solvent ink; corner rounder; pen

yOU caN NOt bE serious...

Okay, so let me get this straight. All the other 5-month old babies are getting dressed up as cute little animals or pumpkins. And me? I get to dress as a penguin. And not just any old penguin mind you, I am Tux the Linux penguin. A mascot for a computer OPERATING SYSTEM! Come on Mom, you couldn't have made me a cowboy costume, or a superhero? I am never going to live this one down.

October 3 | 2003

Great Scrapbook Idea!

Run out of letter stickers? Don't fear, just get creative! With a little bit of brain work, you can piece together many letters by snipping and layering what you have left on the sheet. When Sue ran out of "Es," she simply layered an "F" sticker over an "L" and saved the title! Sometimes you just have to look at things a little differently.

You Can Not Be Serious

Sue Kristoff
Leominster, Massachusetts

Supplies: Cardstock; patterned paper (Reminisce); letter stickers (American Crafts, Doodlebug); chipboard frame, date stamp (Heidi Swapp); chipboard arrow and circle (unknown); pigment ink

Yes, we love Halloween! And we usually have our costumes picked out & chosen months before the actual day. But, I gotta tell ya, we absolutely love the day after Halloween just as much. We always make a special trip to the local Wal-Mart to dig through the piles of leftover costumes. 50 percent off baby!!! And we always come home with some good ones!

THE day after

The Day After

Shannon Taylor
Bristol, Tennessee

Supplies: Cardstock; patterned paper (Artistic Scrapper); letter stickers (American Crafts); ribbon (Offray); wire; spider (artist's own design); Ghostwriter font (Internet download)

Sarah definitely won for height - she stacked her candy on top of itself so she could get more on her cookie. Austin won for originality. He made a karate gingerbread man with a tiny white gi. Harper won for beauty as her house was gorgeous.

It was a party for the kids but it soon turned into a party for the adults. Every year we participate in the Habitat for Humanities Gingerbread Build but this year we couldn't make it. Instead we bought the kits and had a party at home. Soon competitions started to see who could add the most candy to their cookies.

By the end of it we all had tummy aches from sampling too much candy but it was so worth it to have a fun day all together laughing. I am not sure but I think we should make this a yearly tradition.

Magnus who had never seen so much candy in his life spent most of his time sampling it all. He won for consumption!

December 12, 2006

So Who is Having the Most Fun?

Crystal Jeffrey Rieger
Woodbridge, Ontario, Canada

Supplies: Digital paper kit (Oscraps); digital letter brushes (Digi Shop Talk); numbers (7gypsies); rub-on accents (7gypsies, BasicGrey)

A time to spread joy and cheer to others.

A time to reflect and remember blessings.

A time to give and be thankful.

A time to laugh and love with family.

Christmas.
My favorite time of the year.

'Tis the Season

Greta Hammond
Elkhart, Indiana

Supplies: Patterned paper, photo turn (Daisy D's); felt letters, flowers, rhinestones, rub-on letters (Making Memories); rub-on numbers (Autumn Leaves); thread; Bradley Hand font (Microsoft)

Forest to Fabulous

Becky Fleck
Columbus, Montana

Supplies: Cardstock; patterned paper (Chatterbox); letter stickers (American Crafts, KI Memories); acrylic number (KI Memories); die-cut shape (Sizzix); felt, thread; dye ink

Every December, we make our annual trek to the Boulder Canyon to cut a fresh holiday Alpine Fir. Some years, the old, antiquated dirt road has been clear and dry and other years we've found it covered in several feet of snow. This year was definitely the latter. There was so much snow that we fell short of our destined location by almost ten miles. While driving back out of the canyon, we discovered a hidden treasure trove of firs where, really, none should have been growing—several hundred yards from the river's edge, where firs normally make their home. Not only did we find a gloriously perfect tree for Christmas, but it also came complete with a finch's nest tucked deep inside its branches. Mother Nature was the first to place an ornament on this year's tree.

Great Scrapbook Idea!

If you love the look of your Christmas tree but don't want the needles all over your layout, try your hand at this technique: Use a craft knife to slice a sheet of cardstock until you create the look of tree branches. You'll end up with a tree that looks unbelievably real, but without all the mess.

He's So Adorable

Nicole Stark
Roy, Utah

Supplies: Cardstock; chipboard ornaments, patterned paper (BasicGrey); chipboard letters, rhinestones (Heidi Swapp); letter stickers (Making Memories); paint; pigment ink; floss

In helping grandma hang ornaments on the tree you found this cute little snowman. He was made years ago by Aunt Vanessa when she attended preschool. He sure caught you attention and you lovingly cradled him in your hands, not wanting to place him on the tree.

I asked you why you liked him so much and you replied, "He's so adorable!", and then you clasped your hands together.

Believe

Deborah Mahnken
Springfield, Virginia

Supplies: Cardstock; patterned paper (American Crafts, BasicGrey); metal shapes, rub-on letters (Making Memories); flowers (Prima); metal word accent, patterned transparency (K&Co.); spiral clip; staples; stamping ink; diamond glaze (JudiKins); pen

[Ad]ornaments

Becky Fleck
Columbus, Montana

Supplies: Cardstock; patterned paper (Melissa Frances); stone frame (EK Success); ribbons (Shoebox Trims); metal charm (Making Memories); canvas frame (Li'l Davis); acrylic paint; crackle medium; brads, photo turns (7gypsies); dye ink; vellum

the *magic* of christmas

I have to say that I forgot. It was not until you started to figure out that Christmas is magical a season that I remembered. It was not until your eyes lit up from your amazement of it all that I realized what many Christmas holidays as an adult have lacked. It took you, my child, to rekindle the magic in my heart. It took the kindling of yours.

Thanks of the reminder, I needed it.

December 2005

Great Scrapbook Idea!

Even if you don't have the materials to do faux soldering using embossing powder, you can still achieve this look using acrylic paints. Simply squeeze a generous line of gold paint onto a flat surface and dip the edge of your paper or embellishment into the paint. Allow it to dry and then adhere it to your layout. It's that easy!

The Magic of Christmas

Janine Wahl
Sylvan Lake, Alberta, Canada

Supplies: Cardstock; patterned paper (Chatterbox, Flair Designs); letter stickers (American Crafts); rub-on accents (PaperWerx); brads; charms (Li'l Davis); wooden frame (Chatterbox); stamps (Heidi Swapp, Inkadinkado, Plaid); solvent ink; distress ink; pigment ink; dimensional adhesive; acrylic paint; pen

Merry Christmas

Kim Streeter
Vincentia, New South Wales, Australia

Supplies: Cardstock; patterned paper, rub-on accents (BasicGrey); rub-on letters (Making Memories); die-cut shapes (Sizzix); pen

merry
christmas

'06

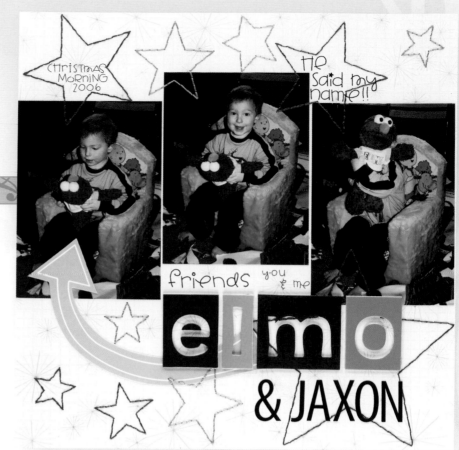

Elmo & Jaxon

Debby Visser
Chilliwack, British Columbia, Canada

Supplies: Patterned paper, chipboard letters (Scenic Route); letter stickers, rub-on letters (Doodlebug); acrylic paint; floss; star template (Dollarstore)

Have Yourselves a Merry Little Christmas

Michele Skinner
Burnsville, Minnesota

Supplies: Cardstock; epoxy stickers, patterned paper, ribbon, rickrack (Making Memories); number stickers (KI Memories); circle cutter; adhesive foam; Merry Script, P22 Garamouche, Palace Script, St. Nicholas, Steelfish, Think Small fonts (Internet download)

Flirting with Santa

Suzy Plantamura
Laguna Niguel, California

Supplies: Cardstock; patterned paper (Hambly, Paper Adventures); chipboard letters (Maya Road); acrylic paint; glitter (Li'l Davis); rub-on accent (Autumn Leaves, Hambly); photo corner (Heidi Swapp); brad; ribbon (unknown); stamping ink; pen

Tom surprised us all by dressing up like Santa on Christmas Eve. When I saw him in that red hunk of a man suit, I had to jump on his lap and give him a kiss!

FLiRTiNG WiTH santa

Christmas! 2006

This was the first Christmas we'd spent with just the four of us in New York City. In fact, this was the first Christmas we'd spent as a family in our own apartment. We had decorated the Christmas tree (mostly with Luca's handmade decorations from school), we'd bought bagels and cream cheese for Christmas morning. I had done my requisite last-minute Ebay/ toysrus.com scramble online, and finally, the day arrived. Luca was thrilled that Santa actually would visit *his* apartment. A few days before Christmas, Luca had asked if the doorman would know to let Santa up…the doormen assured him that they would let him past security. Luca and Julian had alot of fun playing in the box (of course) that one of his larger gifts came in, and Whitten and Mimi's air hockey game was a *huge* hit. (December 2006)

Christmas 2006

Hillary Heidelberg
New York, New York

Supplies: Cardstock; patterned paper (Bo-Bunny); snaps (Making Memories)

Great Scrapbook Idea!

Plaster of Paris doesn't have to be reserved for a kids' art class. Using a snowflake die cut as a mask, Wendy covered strips of cardstock with plaster of Paris. She then removed the die cut and allowed the plaster to dry, adding paint and glitter to dress up her beautiful creation. You can achieve the same look with any shape you can imagine!

Wonder

Wendy J. Mikus
Mesa, Arizona

Supplies: Cardstock; chipboard letters (Li'l Davis); stamps (Rubber Stampede, Technique Tuesday); eyelets (Making Memories); plaster of Paris; acrylic paint; die-cut shapes (unknown); solvent ink; glitter

Snow Day

Kay Rogers
Midland, Michigan

Supplies: Cardstock; frames, patterned paper, ribbon, stickers, tags (KI Memories); pen

Hayden and Ryan

enjoying our

outdoor ice rink

playing

being goofy

cousins & friends

totally having fun!

COLD PLAY

February, 2007

Cold Play

Mary Rogers
Autrain, Michigan

*Supplies: Cardstock; patterned paper,
snowflake accent (BasicGrey); chipboard
letters (Heidi Swapp); distress ink; embossing
powder; corner rounder*

Celebrate Snow

Amanda Williams
Tucson, Arizona

*Supplies: Cardstock; patterned paper (Daisy
D's); chipboard letters (Heidi Swapp); letter
stickers (Creative Imaginations); photo
corners (Heidi Swapp, Making Memories);
acrylic dots (Making Memories); ribbon
(American Crafts); stamping ink; snowflakes
(unknown); thread*

Celebrate snow

On the first day of December
we woke up to a winter
wonderland! Your snowsuit
was way too tight and it was
only 20 degrees outside. The
white powder didn't last for
long, but you certainly
enjoyed the SNOW to its
fullest. You loved the sight,
the feel, and even the taste of
fresh snow. Daddy let you
play outside for as long as
you wanted to. He pulled out
your favorite sled and let you
explore for over an hour!

Now that we've moved to
Arizona, there probably
won't be much snow for
you to play with during
the winter months. I'm
glad you got your first
taste of snow while you
were young. Your mama
and daddy love it, too and
we hope to travel back to
Illinois to let you enjoy
the snow again! 2005

Winter Home

Mary Rogers
Autrain, Michigan

Supplies: Cardstock; patterned paper (BasicGrey); die-cut letters (Provo Craft); stamps (7gypsies, October Afternoon); circle punch; rub-on accent (American Crafts); pen

Snow

Erika Smith
Lorain, Ohio

Supplies: Cardstock; snowflakes (Heidi Swapp); letter stamps (Scrappy Cat); acrylic paint; word stickers (Making Memories); staples; pen

Great Scrapbook Idea!

Don't let your point get lost! Adding just a swipe of paint along the edges of a clear frame and positioning it directly around your intended focal point is a great way to bring the eye to the exact spot you want it to rest. This look can also be achieved with a transparency.

Dreaming of Summer

Crystal Jeffrey Rieger
Woodbridge, Ontario, Canada

Supplies: Cardstock; patterned paper (Chatterbox); transparent frame and letter (Heidi Swapp); acrylic paint; rhinestones; ribbon (Michaels); thread; image editing software (Adobe); corner rounder; pen

Year in Review

Emily Dennis
Hancock, Michigan

Supplies: Patterned paper, chipboard accents, rub-on letters and words (Polar Bear Press); stamping ink; pen

chapter

More than a Princess

Sugar and spice is a thing of the past. Nowadays, girls are doing everything boys are doing and then some. Sure, there's still dance and gymnastics, but there's also soccer and baseball—and that's just to start. Little girls bring big joy and countless scrapbooking opportunities.

From the sports to the tutus, this chapter has a wide array of inspiring ideas to capture the giggles, the grins and even the grimaces with ease! Whether you're preserving the cute things she says or her very first car, all the ideas are right at your fingertips.

Hippy Chick

Yvette Adams
Banks, Australian Capital Territory,
Australia

Supplies: Chipboard letters, letter stickers, patterned paper, ribbon (KI Memories); buttons; floss; photo corner (Heidi Swapp); brads; Susie's Hand font (Internet download)

Ladybug Love

Amy Peterman
Muskegon, Michigan

Supplies: Scalloped cardstock (Bazzill); patterned paper (KI Memories, My Mind's Eye); letter and number stickers (EK Success); letter stamps (Leaving Prints); label stamps (Stampin' Up); sticker accents (7gypsies); rub-on letters and accents (Autumn Leaves, My Mind's Eye); acrylic paint; felt; tulle; floss; buttons (vintage); staples; pen

Daddy: That is a very pretty smile, Ashlyn.

Ashlyn: Yeah. I know. I'm CUTE!

Yes you are baby. You most certainly are.

Great Scrapbook Idea!

Kids say the darndest things! That's why it's important to keep a pen and paper handy at all times—you never know when you're going to overhear a conversation you never want to forget. Once you've got it recorded, save a permanent place in your memory by using the dialogue as the journaling for your next layout. What a great way to make your child the star of the page!

Undeniably Cute

Greta Hammond
Elkhart, Indiana

Supplies: Cardstock; patterned paper (My Mind's Eye); chipboard letters (Li'l Davis); rub-on letters and accents (Doodlebug, Imagination Project); photo corner (Scenic Route); flower (Bazzill); brad (Making Memories); tab (Sizzix); rickrack (Maya Road)

Sweet Alyssa

Gretchen McElveen
Helena, Alabama

Supplies: Cardstock; patterned paper (Junkitz); letter stickers (Doodlebug, Making Memories); ribbon (Li'l Davis); rhinestone heart, transparent heart (Heidi Swapp), staples

M Style

Sandi Minchuk
Merrillville, Indiana

Supplies: Cardstock; scalloped cardstock (Bazzill); patterned paper (Miss Elizabeth's); chipboard letters (Heidi Swapp); letter stickers, quote sticker, velvet ribbon (Making Memories); chalk ink; rickrack (May Arts); circle punch; staples

Great Scrapbook Idea!

Don't be afraid to turn your current photos into classics. If you've got a timeless treasure in your life, pay homage to the olden days by converting a photo of the person to sepia or black and white. You'll see that a layout with an antique style can be both modern and classic.

Timeless

Mary Palmer Chapman
Watertown, South Dakota

Supplies: Patterned paper (K&Co.); chipboard letters (antique letters); tag (office supply store); clock faces (Li'l Davis); watch pieces (removed from broken watch); photo corners (unknown); brads; ribbon (Keeping Memories Alive); pigment ink; pen

Simply Irrestistable

Michelle Marie Liberty
Ocala, Florida

Supplies: Cardstock; patterned paper (Me & My Big Ideas); grommets (Making Memories); chipboard accents (We R Memory Keepers); fibers (BasicGrey); buttons (Chatterbox); vellum; French Script, DB Cutesie Doodles fonts (Internet download)

American Eagle Girls

Susan Hubbs
Orlando, Florida

Supplies: Cardstock; chipboard letters, patterned paper (We R Memory Keepers); charm, rub-on letters (Making Memories); spiral clip (Creative Impressions); ribbon (unknown)

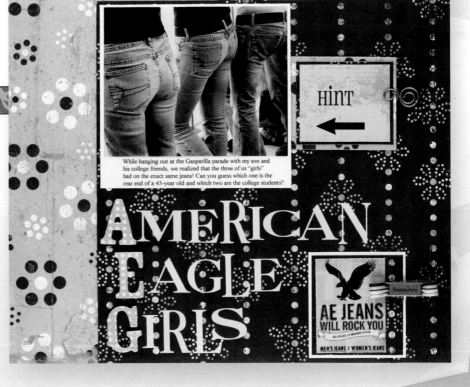

Laugh Every Day

Catherine Feegel-Erhardt
Tampa, Florida

Supplies: Cardstock; patterned paper (Scenic Route); fibers (American Crafts, Coats & Clark, Scraps); paper piercer; pen

Beautifully Breezy

Melita Ganoe
Jacksonville, Florida

Supplies: Patterned paper (BasicGrey); rub-on letters (Making Memories); dye ink; adhesive foam

You have learned so many words + phrases from Sarah. We just love to hear you talk! ☺

My sweet Anna Banana – xu talk non-stop!

I LOVE YOU MUCH

DID YOU HEAR THAT?

LOOK AT ME!

JUICE PLEASE

EXCUSE ME

PLEASE UP

WHAT ARE YOU DOING?

PEEK-A-BOO

SNACK PLEASE

I WANT SARAH!

Anna Banana at 2 yrs.

those things You say...

Great Scrapbook Idea!

Clear embellishments are all the rage, but what if they get lost on your layout? Using acrylic paint along the edges makes a transparent element pop, as does outlining it in a colored marker or pen. Edging is the perfect, subtle look to "clear up" your layouts!

Those Things You Say

Maria Burke
Steinbach, Manitoba, Canada

Supplies: Cardstock; brads, letter stickers, patterned paper (SEI); transparent flowers (Heidi Swapp); stamps (Autumn Leaves, Paper Salon); solvent ink; pen

Natural Beauty

Ann Chapman
Nanaimo, British Columbia, Canada

Supplies: Cardstock; patterned paper (Rhonna Designs, Sandylion); stamps (Rhonna Designs); chalk ink; stamping ink; dimensional adhesive; thread; pen

Your first piggy tails! Mummy was so thrilled that your hair was finally long enough to put up! This is one of my favorite photos. You are a Natural Beauty.

Natural Beauty

What a Girly Girl

Tina Albertson
Harlan, Indiana

Supplies: Cardstock; die-cut shapes and words, patterned paper, transparency frame (My Mind's Eye); chipboard letters, rhinestone border (Heidi Swapp); stamp (Li'l Davis); solvent ink; pen

She

Ria Mojica
Pasig, Metro Manila, Philippines

Supplies: Cardstock; patterned paper (Urban Lily); chipboard letters (Heidi Swapp); word stamps (Paper Salon), butterfly stamp (Technique Tuesday); chalk ink; fibers (BasicGrey); brad (Autumn Leaves); die-cut tag (Sizzix); eyelets; glitter glaze

Great Scrapbook Idea!

Scrapbook pages don't have to be flat! To add some volume, fold an embellishment in half and mount only the center with foam adhesive. This will help the item literally pop right off your page, adding gorgeous depth and dimension.

Cherish

Teri-Lynn Masters
Truro, Nova Scotia, Canada

Supplies: Cardstock; patterned paper (K&Co., Karen Foster, Paper Loft, PSX, unknown); square punch; heart punch; word stamp (Heidi Swapp); solvent ink; adhesive foam; thread; pen

Beautiful Blue Eyes

Rosy Schlitzkus
Bonney Lake, Washington

Supplies: Cardstock; patterned paper (Autumn Leaves, BasicGrey, Boxer Scrapbooks, Close to My Heart, Provo Craft, Scrapworks); stamps (FontWerks); stamping ink; chipboard accents (Making Memories); brads; watercolor pencils; pen

Great Scrapbook Idea!

If you've ever wanted to recreate a watercolor masterpiece, now is your chance! And you don't have to be a painter to do it. Simply ink stamps with a water-based ink and then spray the stamp lightly with water. Stamp onto watercolor paper and trim around the design before adding it to your page. Quick and easy, but beautifully brilliant!

Happy Happy

Rachel Greig
Glenning Valley, New South Wales, Australia

Supplies: Cardstock; watercolor paper; letter stickers, stamps, tags (Making Memories); chipboard letters, flower (Heidi Swapp); brad (Hot Off The Press); stamping ink; acrylic paint; ribbon (unknown); floss

Bathing Beauty

Kay Rogers
Midland, Michigan

Supplies: Cardstock; die-cut letters and shapes, patterned paper, plastic accents, ribbon (KI Memories); pen

Great Scrapbook Idea!

With so many digital products on the market, it's hard not to take notice. Even paper scrapbookers can benefit from the wide array of electronic goodies. Simply download a digital kit and print the background "paper" onto cardstock or photo paper. Now you can incorporate digital products even if you don't want to do most of your scrapping on the computer.

Summer Day

Jody Wilkinson
Bemidji, Minnesota

Supplies: Cardstock; patterned paper (7gypsies, Daisy D's, Rhonna Designs); flower (Prima); picture hangers (Jo-Ann's); ribbon (Offray); rhinestones (My Mind's Eye, Prima); Hurricane font (Internet download)

You Are

Carmen Perez
Corpus Christi, Texas

Supplies: Cardstock; chipboard accents, patterned paper, word accents (Colorbok); chipboard letters and number (Chatterbox); brackets (Paper Loft); bookplate (K&Co.); stamping ink; pen

Suddenly I See

Terri Hayes
Cary, North Carolina

Supplies: Cardstock; scalloped cardstock (Bazzill); patterned paper (American Crafts, Scenic Route); patterned transparency (K&Co.); die-cut letters (Provo Craft); letter stickers (Making Memories); silk flower (Li'l Davis); flower sticker (EK Success); ribbon (May Arts); rub-on trim (Chatterbox); pigment ink; pen

My Girl

Carmen Perez
Corpus Christi, Texas

Supplies: Patterned paper (BasicGrey); chipboard letters (Li'l Davis); chipboard words (Making Memories); velvet accents (SEI); adhesive foam; stamping ink; Sunnydale font (Internet download)

This One

Nicole Harper
Elyria, Ohio

Supplies: Cardstock; patterned paper (American Crafts, Tinkering Ink); letter stickers (EK Success, Heidi Swapp); rub-on trim (American Crafts); acrylic paint; stamp (Stampin' Up); stamping ink; pen

Great Scrapbook Idea!

Get more mileage from your doodling templates! Consider using them to create a guideline for your hand stitching. Lightly trace the doodle you want to use onto your layout and then use a needle or paper piercer to punch holes along the line. Erase the line and stitch the holes with embroidery floss for a funky, hand-made look.

I Love This Girl

Laura Achilles
Littleton, Colorado

Supplies: Cardstock; patterned paper, rub-on flowers (Imagination Project); letter stickers (American Crafts); photo corners, plastic letter, rhinestones (Heidi Swapp); floss

Great Scrapbook Idea!

The next time you're looking for that oh-so-perfect embellishment, look no further than the iron-ons at your local craft store! Iron-ons aren't just for fabric. They make lovely additions to your scrapbook layouts as well, and with a wide variety to choose from, the possibilities are endless.

You

Staci Compher
Carleton, Michigan

Supplies: Patterned paper (Chatterbox, Hot Off The Press); die-cut letters (Daisy D's, Fancy Pants); rub-on accents (BasicGrey); rhinestones (My Mind's Eye); ribbon (Jo-Ann's, May Arts, unknown); label; staples; pen

Great Scrapbook Idea!

For an imperfect but artistic design, paint or ink a mat for your photo rather than matting it on cardstock. This will give your layout an artsy feel and a charming hand-made look. And the process may remind you that you really are an artist.

Diva

Amy Cutler
Irvona, Pennsylvania

Supplies: Cardstock; rub-on accent, transparency (Hambly); letter stamps (Making Memories); index card; typewriter; pigment ink

Smile

Kim Moreno
Tucson, Arizona

Supplies: Cardstock; die-cut letters and shapes, patterned paper, stamp (Sassafras Lass); buttons; pigment ink; floss; pen

Holiday Cheer

Kay Rogers
Midland, Michigan

Supplies: Cardstock; brads, chipboard letters and accents, patterned paper, ribbon, sticker accents (KI Memories); pen

Primavera

Maria Gallardo-Williams
Cary, North Carolina

Supplies: Cardstock; patterned paper (BasicGrey, Fancy Pants); letter stickers (American Crafts); ribbon (Fancy Pants)

Lovely

Sarah Martinez
Rogers, Arkansas

Supplies: Cardstock; word stickers (Bo-Bunny, Three Bugs in a Rug); sticker accents (Making Memories, Three Bugs in a Rug); paper flowers (Prima); brads; adhesive foam; pen

Great Scrapbook Idea!

If you're ever unsatisfied with the color of your photos, you can be thankful you don't have to settle! Using image editing software, you can tint the photos just a bit to acheive a certain color that fits your design scheme. This color change allows for a design that's both attractive and cohesive.

Elizabeth & Eva

Catherine Feegel-Erhardt
Tampa, Florida

Supplies: Cardstock; handmade paper (Magenta); letter stickers (Mrs. Grossman's); ribbons (American Crafts, Offray); charms (Maya Road); thread; pen

Snow Cute

Michelle Coleman
Layton, Utah

Supplies: Digital embellishments, paper, and stamps (Little Dreamer Designs)

Dream Baby

Michelle Cathcart
Sugar Grove, Pennsylvania

Supplies: Cardstock; patterned paper (BasicGrey, KI Memories); chipboard letters and heart (Heidi Swapp); rub-on word (Royal Langnickle); buttons; floss; stamps (Doodlebug); stamping ink; rhinestones; pen

She's got a way about her and everywhere she goes a million dreams of love surround her ♡

Great Scrapbook Idea!

Don't just opt for the patterned paper in the store—create your own! Tape off an area on your cardstock and then stamp within the borders with a watermark ink. Emboss the images in white and then color over the design with the desired chalk color. The result will be a subtle pattern custom-made to perfectly complement the other elements in your layout.

Gabi

Mary MacAskill
Calgary, Alberta, Canada

Supplies: Cardstock; vellum; stamps (Gelatins); watermark ink; embossing powder; chalk; brad, metal accent (Making Memories); button; glossy medium (JudiKins); Sansumi font (Dafont)

gaBi

"A baby will make love stronger, days shorter, nights longer, bankroll smaller, home happier, clothes shabbier, the past forgotten, and the future worth living for."
-unknown-

Sweet

Susan Blanton
Virginia Beach, Virginia

Supplies: Cardstock; patterned paper (Polar Bear Press); stamps (Hero Arts); snaps; solvent ink; circle punch; pen; Typewriter font (Internet download)

Sweet

My Sweet Sydney,
The joy of my Life.
I love you more and
More everyday.
I love your Smile, your
Sweetness, and your heart.

Great Scrapbook Idea!

Scalloped edges are a delightful addition to any page. To ensure that your scallops don't get lost in the mix, dress them up a bit. Adding colorful brads, tiny flowers, little buttons or any other small embellishments allows the scalloped edge to pop rather than simply blend in.

Two Sides

Kay Rogers
Midland, Michigan

Supplies: Cardstock; scalloped cardstock (Bazzill); die-cut letters, patterned paper (Sassafras Lass); letter stickers (Doodlebug); stamps (Autumn Leaves); stamping ink; brads; corner punch; pen

Beautiful

Janneke Smit
Agoura, California

Supplies: Cardstock; patterned paper, word accents (My Mind's Eye); flower charms (Making Memories); floss; date stamp (Staples); pigment ink; paper piercer; chipboard accents (Making Memories); brads; watercolor pencils; pen; Garamond font (Microsoft)

we were browsing our fabric shop when you found this amazing glittery green fabric. "Mommy, we could make a Princess Skirt with this!!" Now I have been looking for a project like this to try out my new sewing machine, but my sewing skills leave very much to be desired.. Still, you loved this fabric and the idea of a beautiful sparkling princess gown so much, that I thought I would give it a try, how hard could it be, right? 3 hours later, and sparkly green glitter everywhere, this is what I came up with. Who knew that tulle was so hard to work with, honestly? It took every ounce of control to not rip out all the seams and try again. Still, you seem to love it, and the sparkling green trail it leaves behind. And I guess that is all that matters.

PRINCESS SKIRT

MAR 11 2007

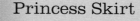

Princess Skirt

Michelle Coleman
Layton, Utah

Supplies: Digital embellishments, paper, and stamps (Little Dreamer Designs)

From Princess to Stinker in Just Three Steps

Alicia Giess
Mansfield, Ohio

Supplies: Cardstock; patterned paper (BasicGrey); letter stamps (Sassafras Lass); stamping ink; lace (Hobby Lobby); decorative scissors; rhinestones (Heidi Swapp); adhesive foam; thread; pen

from princess to stinker in just three steps

Dress her up. Do her hair. Take her out. A 5-year old can only be a princess for a short time before she turns into a little stinker. And I love her that way!

Giggle

Carmen Perez
Corpus Christi, Texas

Supplies: Cardstock; patterned paper, tag and word accents (Sandylion); adhesive foam; brad; stamping ink

Great Scrapbook Idea!

You might not have a lot of time to scrapbook with a new baby in the house, but you better believe you're going to want those vital stats down the road! Create a tag that allows you to record pertinent information after each monthly doctor's visit and fill the tag out monthly. When you're ready to scrap this very busy time in your life, you'll have all the information at your fingertips!

Abby 3 Mo.

Maureen Spell
Muncie, Indiana

Supplies: Digital background, shadow actions (Funky Playground Designs); digital button, journaling card, stamped letters, tulle (Jen Wilson); flower (Scrapbook Graphics); cross-stitch, date stamp, grunge overlay, stitched notecard (Designer Digitals); Dirty Ego, Traveling Typewriter font (Dafont)

Great Scrapbook Idea!

All the text on your page tells the story. But sometimes it's important for just a few certain words to be the center of attention. To make a word stand out, dab a thin line of dimensional adhesive over it. The result is a subtle shine that begs to be noticed.

Bloopers

Caroline Huot
Laval, Quebec, Canada

Supplies: Cardstock; patterned paper (Paper Adventures); rub-on letters (Bobarbo, Imagination Project); rickrack (May Arts); epoxy stickers, micro beads, rhinestones (Dollarama); flowers (Prima); label words (Paper Loft); tab (Die Cuts With A View); Diamond Glaze (JudiKins); pigment ink; Arial, Georgia fonts (Microsoft)

Cheesy Grin

Michelle Coleman
Layton, Utah

Supplies: Digital embellishments, paper, and stamps (Little Dreamer Designs)

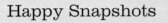

All Done

Julie Kelley
Tewksbury, Massachusetts

Supplies: Digital embellishments, letters and paper (Shabby Princess); image editing software (Adobe); Butik, Kid Typer Ruled fonts (Internet download)

Happy Snapshots

Sarah Martinez
Rogers, Arkansas

Supplies: Patterned paper (7gypsies, Scenic Route); transparency (My Mind's Eye); letter stickers (American Crafts, EK Success); chipboard word, decorative tape, photo corners (Heidi Swapp); clip (Making Memories); stamps (Heidi Swapp, Stampin' Up); pigment ink; pen

Strike a Pose

Emily Dennis
Hancock, Michigan

Supplies: Cardstock; patterned paper, rub-on letters and accents (Polar Bear Press); letter stickers (American Crafts); transparent heart (Heidi Swapp); date sticker (7gypsies); ribbon (unknown); brads; staples; thread; pen

125

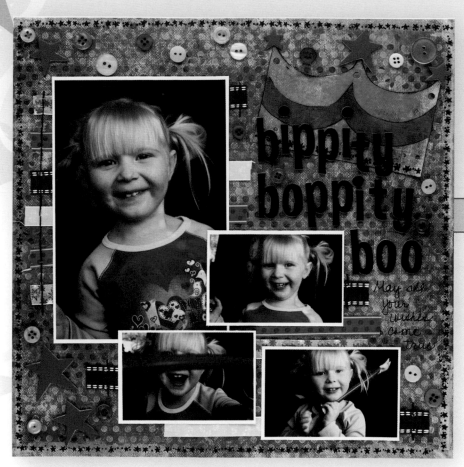

Davinie Fiero
Redmond, Oregon

Supplies: Chipboard stars, patterned paper, ribbon, stamps (Fancy Pants); chipboard letters (American Crafts); buttons (Autumn Leaves); floss; acrylic paint; thread; pen

Princess of Ham-a-lot

Heather Dewaelsche
Fishers, Indiana

Supplies: Cardstock; flower brads, patterned paper, ribbon (Making Memories); paper flowers (Prima); silk flowers (Hirschberg Schutz); rhinestones (Making Memories, Westrim); Black Chancery, Swenson fonts (Internet download)

Laura Achilles
Littleton, Colorado

Supplies: Cardstock; patterned paper (Dream Street); chipboard and rub-on letters (Imagination Project); pigment ink; acrylic paint; pen

Great Scrapbook Idea!

Love the look of scalloped edges, but not sure how to get it? If you've got a heart, teardrop or circle punch handy, you've got all you need. Simply punch cardstock into one of these shapes and then place the shapes in a row under another sheet of patterned paper or cardstock, leaving only the tops exposed. The result is a flawless scallop every time.

Her Lovie

Shannon Brouwer
Gilbert, Arizona

Supplies: Cardstock; patterned paper (Sassafras Lass); letter stickers (Creative Imaginations); rub-on letters (Doodlebug); canvas tabs (Scrapworks); chipboard swirls (Maya Road); flower accents (Heidi Swapp); buttons (Buttons Galore, Making Memories); chalk ink; adhesive foam; 2Peas Quirky font (Two Peas in a Bucket)

The joy you express when visiting the gardens just warms my heart. You are so happy looking at the plants, checking out the koi in the pond, and running through the spray park. There is always some new aspect of nature to discover. I hope you always maintain that sense of wonder, bean!

Discover

Wonder

JOY

Joy

Kay Rogers
Midland, Michigan

Supplies: Decorative tape, letter stickers, patterned paper, ribbon, sticker accents (Making Memories); flowers (Prima); brads; stamping ink

Audrey Quinn, at just three months old you already have such a range of expressions—these photos were taken in just a few minutes and look at all the stories you are telling with your face. It makes me wonder what you will do with your life someday—what you will do, who you will be. I know that I will probably always have an opinion on things, but I promise to try and let you follow your heart's desire. So, be a doctor or a lawyer, be an actor, be an artist, be a writer, be a dental hygienist, be a mom, be a single gal, be a traveler, be a seeker, be a teacher, be a student... whatever you do, my sweet...

be audrey

Be Audrey

Lisa Kisch
Ottawa, Ontario, Canada

Supplies: Cardstock; patterned paper (Chatterbox, My Mind's Eye); rub-on accents (American Crafts); mosaic tiles; rickrack; staples

Great Scrapbook Idea!

Sometimes the ideal patterned paper isn't patterned paper at all! Gift wrap and quilting fabrics also make beautiful backgrounds for your layouts. You might even try a bit of batting for added dimension, upping the "touchability factor" of your layout. Don't be afraid to raid other sections of the craft store. You might be surprised at what little treasures you find waiting for you!

Beautiful Spirit

Amy Peterman
Muskegon, Michigan

Supplies: Cardstock; patterned paper (Old Navy, Scenic Route); rub-on letters (EK Success); rub-on accents (Chatterbox); patterned transparency (My Mind's Eye); ribbon (Making Memories); rickrack (Karen Foster); tag (Rusty Pickle); brads; fabric; quilt batting; staples; pen

She is Beautiful

Courtney Kelly
Anchorage, Alaska

Supplies: Cardstock; patterned paper (Scenic Route); word stamps (Magnetic Poetry); flowers (Heidi Swapp, Prima); sequins (Doodlebug); adhesive foam

Silly Sally

Michelle Coleman
Layton, Utah

Supplies: Digital embellishments, paper, and stamps (Little Dreamer Designs)

Got Wheels

Jane Davies
Westbank, British Columbia, Canada

Supplies: Cardstock; chipboard letters, die-cut shapes, patterned paper (Piggy Tales); letter stickers (American Crafts); chipboard accent (Maya Road); rub-on accents (Autumn Leaves, Doodlebug, My Mind's Eye); brads; glossy topcoat (Ranger)

Always Sunshine

Amy Peterman
Muskegon, Michigan

Supplies: Cardstock; patterned paper (Autumn Leaves, Imagination Project, Rusty Pickle, Scrapworks); letter stickers (EK Success); chipboard accents (Imagination Project); plastic letters (KI Memories); acrylic paint; brads; conchos (Scrapworks); felt; floss; ribbon (unknown); staples; transparency; pen

Great Scrapbook Idea!

Give your photos a translucent look by printing them on a transparency. This creative technique is a fun way to acheive a completely different look for your layouts and allows you to experiment with a number of backgrounds for your photos. Patterned paper, colored cardstock even textured ribbon will show through a transparency, changing the look of your photos in a snap.

Sam

Janet Poelsma
Bradenton, Florida

Supplies: Cardstock; patterned paper, rub-on letters and words (BasicGrey); large flower (Heidi Swapp); plastic flower (Queen & Co.); other flowers (Prima); brads; photo turns; dye ink; pen

First Steps

Heather Verrier
Grimsby, Ontario, Canada

Supplies: Cardstock; patterned paper (Imagination Project, Scrapworks); transparent letters (Heidi Swapp); acrylic paint; chipboard letters and shapes (artist's own design), stamps (Gelatins); sticker accents (Provo Craft); tag (Me & My Big Ideas); pen

sweetie pie

You were mobile from an early age but it seemed that it took you a while to finally take those **first steps**. At first you loved riding around on your walker in the kitchen. You took your **first steps** just after your first birthday (February 15th). At the end of March, you were taking about **3-4 steps** at a time and you were totally walking by the end of April.

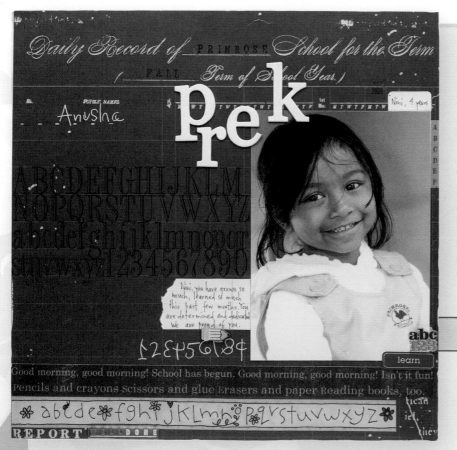

Great Scrapbook Idea!

You may think you'll never forget the adorable chicken scratches of a child who is just learning to write, but don't take any chances! Consider sectioning off a spot on a layout where you can feature your child's developing handwriting as a way to preserve this precious stage in her life. If you're not confident she'll stay within her little spot, add a separate sheet of paper or slip of cardstock to the design after she writes.

Pre K

Mou Saha
Tampa, Florida

Supplies: Cardstock; patterned paper (AdornIt, Autumn Leaves, Making Memories); chipboard letters (Zsiage); metal and gel accents (Making Memories); stamp (Provo Craft); stamping ink; rub-on letters and numbers (Heidi Swapp); pen

Kinder

Shirley Chai
Ringwood, Victoria, Australia

Supplies: Chipboard accents and letters, die-cut card, patterned paper, ribbon (Fancy Pants); epoxy stickers (Autumn Leaves); stamping ink; pen

Beaming with Pride

Maria Burke
Steinbach, Manitoba, Canada

Supplies: Patterned paper, letter stickers, rub-on accents (SEI); stamps (Autumn Leaves, Paper Salon); solvent ink; chipboard star (Deluxe Designs); corner rounder; circle cutter

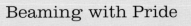

Getting Glasses

Michelle Coleman
Layton, Utah

Supplies: Digital papers, stamps and embellishments (Little Dreamer Designs)

Today you went to the doctor to have a check up and update your shots. As a reward for your braveness, you were given this special Tinkerbell sticker by a nurse in the office!

January 17th, 2007

Great Scrapbook Idea!

It's likely you've got tons of alphabet stickers in your stash, but maybe you're tired of using them in the conventional way. Why not create a mask for your next title by adhering letter stickers and then painting over them? Once the paint is applied, carefully remove the stickers and admire the stunning results!

Your Sticker Reward

Amy Hummel
St. George, Utah

Supplies: Cardstock; patterned paper (Sassafras Lass, Scenic Route); acrylic paint; letter stickers (American Crafts); brads; transparency; pen

My Favorite Things

Michelle Coleman
Layton, Utah

Supplies: Digital embellishments, paper, and stamps (Little Dreamer Designs)

JULY 2006

Clara, you know I love books, that's really no secret. And nothing pleases me more than to see your love of books grow. Alex loved books even from the very beginning, but you were a different story. You fussed and fidgeted in our arms as we read to you even as a tiny infant. But we continued to read, we never gave up. You may have been wandering around your room, playing with your toys as we read, but we didn't stop. Now, just lately, I can see it beginning to pay off. You are beginning your own love affair with books and the stories they contain. You have favorites we read over and over, you have familiar characters that have become your friends and you and Alex reinact your some of your favorite stories in play. You pile books in your bed before going to sleep to look at, occasionally falling asleep with one still in your hands. It excites me to no end to watch this happen and for you to see how much joy and adventure are to be found in books when you...

READ

THE WORLD IS BUT A CANVAS TO THE IMAGINATION.

Read

Tracie Radtke
Chicago, Illinois

Supplies: Digital kit (Shabby Shoppe); Arial, Arial Black fonts (Microsoft)

Bookworm

Lisa Botte
North Billerica, Massachusetts

Supplies: Patterned paper (Making Memories, Me & My Big Ideas); chipboard letters, letter stamps (Making Memories); chipboard accents (BasicGrey, Making Memories); plastic letters (unknown); library pocket (Autumn Leaves); decorative scissors; ribbon (Michaels, Morex); photo corners (Heidi Swapp); acrylic paint; stamping ink; pen

One of Her Habits

Nicole Harper
Elyria, Ohio

Supplies: Cardstock; patterned paper (Making Memories); letter stickers (American Crafts, EK Success, Heidi Swapp, Making Memories); journaling card (Jenni Bowlin); rub-on letters (American Crafts); date stamp (Catslife Press); paper trim (Doodlebug); stamping ink; staples; pen

One Happy Girl

Cathy Schellenberg
Steinbach, Manitoba, Canada

Supplies: Cardstock; patterned paper (Die Cuts With A View); letter stickers (SEI); stamps (Autumn Leaves); acrylic paint; stamping ink; sandpaper; Café Rojo font (Internet download)

WITH THE SUN SHINING ON YOUR FACE,
THE WIND BLOWING THROUGH YOUR HAIR,
YOUR FIRST TUBE RIDE UNDER YOUR BELT
AND THE PROMISE
OF A LONG, SUNNY DAY AT THE BEACH,
YOU ARE

one happy girl

The Imaginative Child

Alison Lockett
Knoxville, Tennessee

Supplies: Cardstock; patterned paper (Bam Pop); chipboard stars, letter stickers (American Crafts); buttons (Die Cuts With A View); stamp (Sassafras Lass); rub-on accents (7gypsies, BasicGrey); pen

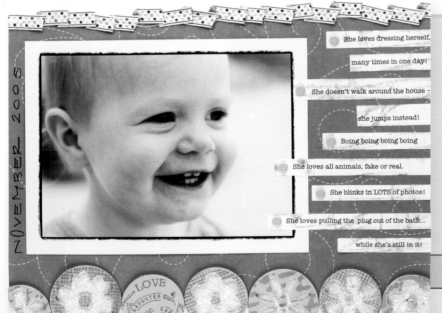

Great Scrapbook Idea!

Chipboard comes in just about every color, but that shouldn't stop you from dressing it up even more! Stamps, glitter, paint, paper, even your favorite set of markers can all change the appearance of chipboard. What an inexpensive and fun way to add that little something extra to your layout!

Zoe's Quirks

Rachel Greig
Glenning Valley, New South Wales, Australia

Supplies: Cardstock; patterned paper (KI Memories); chipboard accents, ribbon (Maya Road); letter stamps (Creative Imaginations, Penny Black, Stamp-It); snaps; acrylic paint; glitter glue; stamping ink; pen

Great Scrapbook Idea!

There are so many ways to use your computer while you're scrapbooking! One fun thing you can do is to create a template on your computer, complete with photos, journaling headlines and a title. Then, remove your photo markers and print the page onto a sheet of cardstock. You can add your photos along with your own handwriting for a clever and adorable end result!

5 Year Old Fact Sheet

Kim Frantz
Oxford, Pennsylvania

Supplies: Cardstock; patterned paper (Rusty Pickle); chipboard tag (American Crafts); brads, number stickers (Making Memories); rickrack; flower punches (EK Success); acrylic paint; adhesive foam; pen; Helvetica Neue, Impact fonts (Microsoft)

I Believe I Can Fly

Michelle Coleman
Layton, Utah

Supplies: Digital embellishments, paper, and stamps (Little Dreamer Designs)

Bunny Love

Nicole Harper
Elyria, Ohio

Supplies: Patterned paper (Cosmo Cricket, FontWerks); acrylic paint; rub-on letters (CherryArte, Making Memories); sticker accent (7gypsies); staples; pen

Great Scrapbook Idea!

Cutting that perfect circle is no easy task, especially when you're hoping to create an extra large shape. Next time you need a template for your layout, consider using something on hand, like a dinner plate or embroidery hoop, both of which come in a variety of sizes. Cutting perfect circles has never been so easy!

Spectacular Ride

Amy Hummel
St. George, Utah

Supplies: Cardstock; patterned paper, rub-on words (Scenic Route); hand cut flowers; brads; corner rounder; pigment ink; pen

Let Her Eat Cake

Karlyn Lokken
Lewes, Delaware

Supplies: Cardstock; patterned paper (Imagination Project, KI Memories); die-cut letters (KI Memories); rub-on letters (Imagination Project); brads, sequin flowers (Queen & Co.); decorative tape, journaling tag (Heidi Swapp); paper trim (Doodlebug); plastic frame (Scrapworks); chipboard circle; rub-on accent (Fancy Pants); pen

Happy Helper

Roxanne Jegodtka
Sherwood Park, Alberta, Canada

Supplies: Cardstock; patterned paper (American Crafts); chipboard letters (Heidi Swapp); brads; circle cutter; paper glaze (Duncan); pen

She

Grace Castillo
Anaheim, California

Supplies: Cardstock; patterned paper (My Mind's Eye); chipboard word, journaling tags, plastic and rub-on flowers, photo corner, rhinestone (Heidi Swapp); sticker accent (7gypsies); letter stamps (Making Memories); brad (Queen & Co.); pen

Chalk

May Flaum
Vacaville, California

Supplies: Cardstock; patterned paper (Autumn Leaves, Daisy D's, Luxe Designs); rub-on letters (Mustard Moon); flowers (Bazzill); ribbon (American Crafts, Heidi Grace); photo corners (American Crafts); chipboard shapes (Scenic Route); brads; rub-on accents (BasicGrey); stamping ink; corner rounder; pen

Behind Your Eyes

Laura Achilles
Littleton, Colorado

Supplies: Cardstock; patterned paper, ribbon, tag (We R Memory Keepers); chipboard letters (Heidi Swapp); pen; Pea Kelly font (Internet download)

They say the eyes are the windows of the soul. When I look at this picture I wonder what Allison is thinking and feeling. What is it that is so important to her? What are her goals, her dreams, her desires. Yes, she is young but she has a bright future and bright hope for tomorrow. Where will this path called life lead her? I wish I could go inside her head right now and discover the whole other world inside of her and see what she sees, think what she thinks and hear the things she hasn't said.

A Beauty

Kim Christensen
Fair Oaks, California

Supplies: Digital buttons, paper, safety pin, small flowers, staples, stitching (ScrapArtist); brads, flowers (My Digital Muse); small buttons (Designer Digitals); felt heart, tag (LilyPad); DSP Pollyanna, Susie's Hand fonts (Internet download)

Freestyle Girl

Maria Burke
Steinbach, Manitoba, Canada

Supplies: Cardstock; patterned paper (BasicGrey, Karen Foster, SEI); label, letter stickers (SEI); chipboard monkey (We R Memory Keepers); acrylic paint; stamp (Autumn Leaves); solvent ink; Café Rojo font (Internet download)

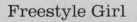

freestyle girl

GO WITH THE FLOW

a TOTAL RIOT

monkey PANTS

FLY BY THE SEAT OF YOUR PANTS

TOTALLY CAREFREE

June 18/06
Sarah @ MHV

Getting What She Wants

first she tries charm...

whining doesn't generally work, but it's worth a try...

maybe

Mom will give in for a pout...

the magic word often

helps, "PLEASE!"

ESME · SUMMER 2005

Great Scrapbook Idea!

We're all looking to save a few dollars so it makes sense to look for ways for products to pull double duty on a layout. The next time you think about using library cards or other types of cards as photo mats, consider also using them as journaling blocks. This not only saves you space, but it creates an unexpected design for the page!

Getting What She Wants

Jenny Adams Powers
Holyoke, Massachusetts

Supplies: Patterned paper (Provo Craft); die-cut letters (Sizzix); library cards (Top Notch); rickrack (Wrights); staples; epoxy stickers, transparency (Creative Imaginations); photo corners; labels (Dymo); pen

Party Girl

Katrina Huerta
Glendale, Arizona

Supplies: Cardstock; die-cut shapes, patterned paper (Sassafras Lass); chipboard letters, foam brackets (American Crafts); photo corner, transparent heart (Heidi Swapp); plastic hearts (Heidi Grace); pigment ink; pen

Two-year-olds on a princess scooter – who could ask for more entertainment than that?! You girls were hilarious trying to help each other figure out how the scooter worked. You probably could not understand why we (moms) were laughing so hard – you were just TOO CUTE!

There were several times both of you got a little speed and rode for a short distance – I couldn't believe how excited you were! Caroline, one time you were so excited you did a happy dance! You girls are the best of friends, and you have tons of fun together – but this was one of the best adventures!

Teamwork

Holly Pittroff
Mooresville, North Carolina

Supplies: Cardstock; patterned paper (American Crafts); chipboard letters (Pressed Petals); chipboard accents (Deluxe Designs, Maya Road); rickrack (May Art); stamping ink; adhesive foam; pen; Goudita Sans font (Internet download)

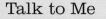

Talk to Me

Kay Rogers
Midland, Michigan

Supplies: Cardstock; brads, patterned paper, ribbon, sticker frame (Making Memories); letter stickers (EK Success); flowers (Prima); corner rounder

You have become a master storyteller. And sometimes, my dear, the talk is pure fiction. Like when daddy asked you how the crayon got all over your sunglasses. Your answer? "The crayon just fell on the glasses, daddy!" And when we asked who drew on the walls, your answer was "Whizzy did." Now I'm not sure how a tiny cat clutched a crayon in her paw and managed to draw 4 feet up a wall, but in your mind it made perfect sense. Eventually you admit what happened, and I'm sure this "creativity" with the truth will pass soon enough. In the meantime, baby girl, talk to me. I love to hear your thoughts. Always.

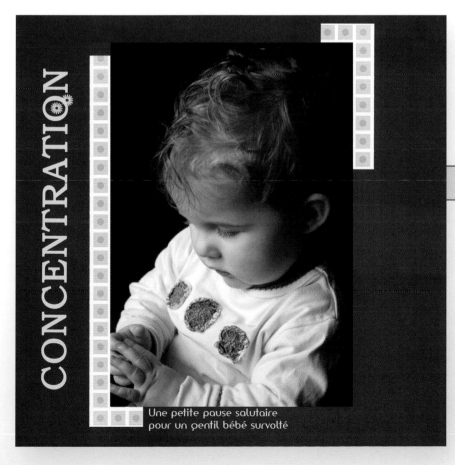

Concentration

Champagne Severine
Dolomieu, France

Supplies: Digital cardstock (ScrapArtist); patterned paper (Atomic Cupcake); brush (Just Lia); image editing software (Adobe); Amerika Sans font (Internet download); Bookman Old Style font (Microsoft)

Wishes for You

Jennifer A. Davis
Woodruff, Wisconsin

Supplies: Cardstock; flower, rickrack (Prima); journaling tag (7gypsies); word sticker (Making Memories); label sticker (Dymo); brads; button; staples; lace (unknown); corner rounder; pen

Lara Camille

Tish Treadaway
Harrisburg, North Carolina

Supplies: Cardstock; patterned paper, sticker accents (Bo-Bunny); chipboard word (Li'l Davis); flowers (Prima); patterned transparency (My Mind's Eye); rickrack (BasicGrey); decorative scissors

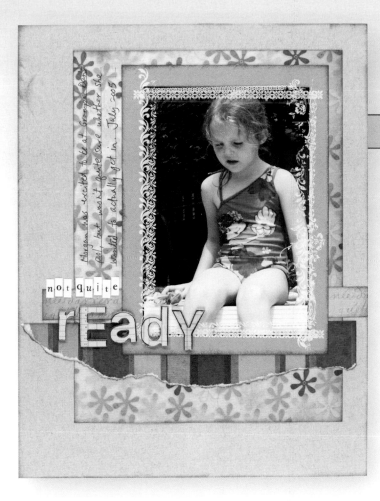

Not Quite Ready

Liz Goldhawk
London, Ontario, Canada

Supplies: Cardstock; patterned paper (7gypsies); chipboard letters (Heidi Swapp); letter stickers (Making Memories); rub-on frame (Daisy D's); chalk ink; pen

Great Scrapbook Idea!

Every once in a while, we stumble upon a piece of patterned paper that is too beautiful to completely cover. If you love the design of a sheet of paper, why not incorporate it into your photograph? Simply cut around the paper's design element you want to showcase and slide the top of your photo underneath. This technique adds beauty as well as dimension to your layout.

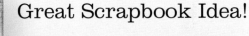

Alayna

Kim Hughes
Roy, Utah

Supplies: Patterned paper (BasicGrey, Creative Impressions, K&Co., Scenic Route); patterned transparency (My Mind's Eye); chipboard letters (American Crafts); rub-on accents (Bo-Bunny); lace (unknown); ribbon (Offray); flower (Prima); buttons (Autumn Leaves); photo turn (Queen & Co.); brad; pigment ink; thread; pen

Great Scrapbook Idea!

If you find yourself with a photograph that has a good deal of empty space, don't crop it, use it! That empty space is the perfect spot for your journaling. You can either electronically journal onto the photo before printing it out, or you can simply use a permanent marker or gel pen to handwrite your stories for stellar results.

She's Got Spunk

Amy Peterman
Muskegon, Michigan

Supplies: Patterned paper (Imagination Project, Making Memories); rub-on accents (KI Memories); acrylic paint; clip, ribbon (Making Memories); decorative scissors; transparency; staples; pen; Chivalry font (Internet download)

Biker Chic

Lisa Jamerson
Evington, Virginia

Supplies: Cardstock; patterned paper (Scenic Route); chipboard letters (Imagination Project); flowers (Prima); rub-on accent (American Crafts); brads; acrylic paint; flower mask (Heidi Swapp); photo turns (7gypsies); dimensional adhesive

Rock Star

Shirley Chai
Ringwood, Victoria, Australia

Supplies: Chipboard letters and stars, patterned paper, rub-on word, stamps (Li'l Davis); rhinestone frame (Heidi Swapp); eyelets; pen

Rock On

Michelle Lanning
La Habra, California

Supplies: Cardstock; patterned paper (Scenic Route); journaling paper (Creative Imaginations); letter stickers (American Crafts); acrylic paint; pigment ink; chalk; buttons; pen

Explore

Becky Chabot
Sanford, Maine

Supplies: Cardstock; patterned paper (BasicGrey); letter stencils (Bazzill); decorative tape (Heidi Swapp); decorative punches (Creative Memories, Marvy); brads; labels (Brother); transparency film (3M); nameplate (ArtQuest); buttons (unknown); thread

Found Treasure

Kay Rogers
Midland, Michigan

Supplies: Cardstock; scalloped cardstock (Bazzill); die-cut letters and tags, patterned paper (Crate Paper); letter stickers (EK Success); ribbon (SEI); stamp (Autumn Leaves); stamping ink; dimensional adhesive; pen

Great Scrapbook Idea!

Ways to add photos and journaling to your layouts abound, you just have to look for them! Even a small embellishment can become a mini-album that hides a few tiny photos and the story behind them. You'll save space and add some clever details to your layout.

Bug Ladies

Catherine Feegel-Erhardt
Tampa, Florida

Supplies: Cardstock; patterned paper (Rusty Pickle, artist's own design); chipboard letters, ladybug embellishment (EK Success); paint; decoupage medium; brads; photo turns, ribbon (unknown); stamping ink; thread; pen

She's One Tough Princess

Crystal Jeffrey Rieger
Woodbridge, Ontario, Canada

Supplies: Cardstock; patterned paper (SEI); letter stickers (Making Memories); rhinestone letters and accents (Prima); button; flower (Wal-Mart); felt; photo corner (Trace Industries); pen

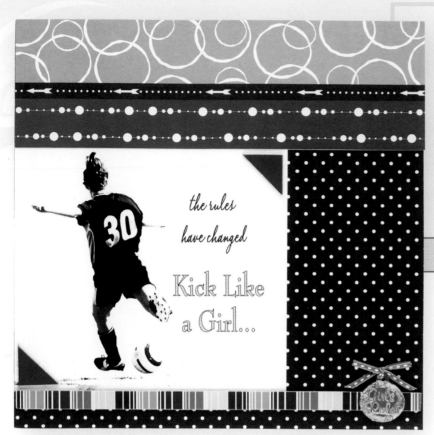

Great Scrapbook Idea!

To ensure that your photos really pack a punch, consider eliminating the background, putting all the attention on the element you most want to showcase. With nothing in the background to distract it, the eye is free to focus on the photo's subject. The results are pictures that really make a statement!

Kick Like a Girl

Susan Hubbs
Orlando, Florida

Supplies: Chipboard accent, patterned paper (Scenic Route); metal charm (Happy Hammer); ribbon (Susan's Scrapbook Shack); Bernhardt Mod, Pegsanna fonts (Internet download)

Fire Starter

Crystal Jeffrey Rieger
Woodbridge, Ontario, Canada

Supplies: Cardstock; patterned paper (BasicGrey); chipboard letters (Scenic Route); die-cut shapes (My Mind's Eye); felt flowers (Dollarstore); felt flourish (Blueye Dezines); ribbon (Michaels); acrylic paint; brads; buttons; staples; pen

Dance

Lisa Tutman-Oglesby
Mundelein, Illinois

Supplies: Cardstock; definition accent, flower, patterned paper, ribbon (Making Memories); chipboard letter (Heidi Swapp); large flower (Michaels); brads; rub-on accents (BasicGrey); stamp (Creative Imaginations); circle punch; decorative scissors; corner rounder; stamping ink; thread

My Shoes, Your Shoes

Yvette Adams
Banks, Australian Capital
Territory, Australia

Supplies: Cardstock; patterned paper (Sandylion); chipboard shapes, photo corner, rub-on letters (Heidi Swapp); rub-on accents (BasicGrey); tag; ribbon; buttons; corner rounder; thread; pen; Century Gothic font (Microsoft)

Great Scrapbook Idea!

There are so many ways to journal on a layout, but many don't allow for long-winded thoughts. If you're looking for a way to include a high word count, consider hiding your journaling in a booklet. Here, Tiffany was able to write more words without overwhelming her design by including her journaling underneath the photo.

Reach for the Sky

Tiffany Gallegos
Houston, Texas

Supplies: Cardstock; patterned paper (Creative Imaginations, K&Co.); hinges (Daisy D's); ribbon (Offray); thread; flowers (unknown); Adine Kirnberg, Antique Type, Champagne, Migraine Sans fonts (Internet download); Flower Garden, Willie Mac Dividers I accents (Internet download)

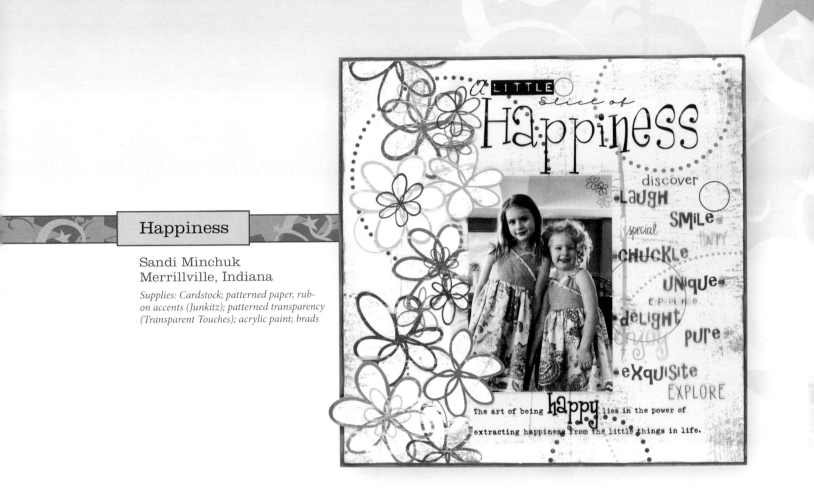

Happiness

Sandi Minchuk
Merrillville, Indiana

Supplies: Cardstock; patterned paper, rub-on accents (Junkitz); patterned transparency (Transparent Touches); acrylic paint; brads

Wishes

Sandi Minchuk
Merrillville, Indiana

Supplies: Cardstock; patterned paper (Autumn Leaves, Sassafras Lass); quote sticker (Memories Complete); bird sticker (Autumn Leaves)

chapter

More than Prince Charming

They bring bugs in the house. They jump in mud puddles
in their brand new dress shoes. They shove rolls and
rolls of toilet paper down the toilet just to see what will
happen. And they give the best hugs. Boys are equal
parts sweet, cute and full of mischief, and therefore, they
make excellent subjects for your scrapbooking projects.
Whether they're playing sports, digging in the yard or
growing up way too fast, this chapter has a variety of
ideas for scrapbooking the big and little boys in your life.
Leaving no stone unturned, this chapter looks at all facets
of those princely children at every stage of the journey.

Great Scrapbook Idea!

We all know boys like mud, but adding real mud to your layouts would be a bit messy! To simulate a dirty, muddy look on your next page, spray texture paint onto an embellishment or sheet of cardstock. Then cover it with brown acrylic paint. The texture paint will show through to create mud splats that look true to life.

Boys Will Be

Kathlynn Hughes
Stevenson Ranch, California

Supplies: Patterned paper (Cloud 9); chipboard letters (Heidi Swapp); texture spray (Krylon); acrylic paint; die-cut shapes (Ellison); patterned transparency (Transparent Touches)

No Girls in this World

Michele Skinner
Burnsville, Minnesota

Supplies: Cardstock; patterned paper (Cloud 9, KI Memories, My Mind's Eye); letter and word stickers (American Crafts, KI Memories, Making Memories); watermark ink; brads; cutting templates (Crafter's Workshop, EK Success); corner rounder; pen

Mtn. Boy

Kim Moreno
Tucson, Arizona

Supplies: Cardstock; patterned paper (Piggy Tales); chipboard letters (Bazzill); chipboard accent (Technique Tuesday); digital image (Holly VanDyne); transparency; pigment ink; stamps (FontWerks); staples; pen

Great Scrapbook Idea!

Don't let inches dictate where your layout ends. Consider allowing portions of your layout to hang off the edge of the page, adding a fun twist to a typical scrapbook design. With the size of your layout a bit unusual, you'll add visual interest and dimension to even a simple page.

Boys

Courtney Walsh
Winnebago, Illinois

Supplies: Brads, letter stickers, patterned paper (Chatterbox); pigment ink; floss; pen

Great Scrapbook Idea!

Who says digital scrapbooking is impersonal? Adding your own touches is a snap! To include your digital handwriting, simply write your text in a black pen or marker and scan the image. Using image editing software, simply copy the image and paste it onto your layout for a personal, one-of-a-kind addition to your page.

Autumn is Here: Time to Play

Janine Wahl
Sylvan Lake, Alberta, Canada

Supplies: Digital elements (artist's own design); image editing software (Microsoft); Arial, Century Gothic, Times New Roman fonts (Microsoft); Busy Babs, CopperCanyonWBW fonts (Internet download)

He is a Saver

Brenda McAndrews
Villa Hills, Kentucky

Supplies: Cardstock; patterned paper (Arctic Frog, Bo-Bunny); brads; dye ink; pen; ABC Teacher font (Internet download); Century Gothic, Edwardian Script fonts (Microsoft)

Perpetual Motion

Sara Wise
Wasilla, Alaska

Supplies: Cardstock; chipboard accent, patterned paper, stamps (Sassafras Lass); labels (Dymo); letter stickers (AdornIt); rub-on star (Polar Bear Press); tag (Doodlebug); dye ink; brads; pen

Sorry, Henry, but it's true. You are a geek. A bit of a nerd. And no matter what people may say as you get older, that really isn't a bad thing. I mean, really ... geeks and nerds rule the world. And quite honestly, I don't think you mind a bit. You have no qualms about telling people you want to build robots and create video games. Your favorite afterschool activity isn't a sport, it's Mad Science. Even when class is over, I have to literally drag you out because you want to stay and talk to the teacher and help her clean up.

That's awesome, kid.

You are only seven and yet you have a fourth grade reading level and a clear aptitude for science and technology, and yet your teacher says math is the subject that comes most naturally to you. Wow, Henry. You will go far in your life if you always embrace knowledge and place importance on intelligence and cheer on your inner geek.

And while being all-around brilliant can be seen as geeky by some, it is your hobbies that will truly define you. You love the Star Wars movies. You love Sci-Fi. You would rather play X-Box with Daddy or your Gameboy than baseball with the neighbor kids. You don't ask if you can play with your toys, you ask if you can do an experiment with your science kits. You dig up bugs not to squish them or light them on fire, but to study them. You hum classical music. Or "Video Killed the Radio Star."

H, you are a geek. And you get it honestly. Daddy and I are definitely geeky, though we managed to balance it with sports, too. I hope you keep up soccer and swimming and taekwondo. You may need to know how to defend yourself someday against some jock who says being a geek is a bad thing. Pull a sparring move on him, then grab your chemistry set and head off happily to MIT to build robots. Just like you say you want to do.

And never forget that geeks rule the world. Because you, my friend, will be just fine.

Geeking Out

Michele Skinner
Burnsville, Minnesota

Supplies: Cardstock; patterned paper (KI Memories, Scenic Route); floss; stitching template (Li'l Davis); pen; Century Gothic font (Microsoft); Po Beef font (Internet download)

Great Scrapbook Idea!

If you're tired of the same old title treatment, look no further than your patterned paper for inspiration. By mimicking an existing pattern and incorporating it into your title, you're sure to create a cohesive design every time!

Greta Hammond
Elkhart, Indiana

Supplies: Cardstock; chipboard shapes, patterned paper (Imagination Project); chipboard letters (Heidi Swapp, Imagination Project); brads; corner rounder

From the moment you saw it, you were completely and utterly enthralled. Grandma had sent this Spiderman costume in hopes that you might like it. Well, it quickly became your uniform and I had to pry it off of you to wash every few days. You would wear it day in and day out and I finally had to put my foot down when you would try to leave the house in it! It is now faded and paper thin with holes in the knees and some of the seams. It is about 3 inches too short but you still try to wear it occasionally. It has been a favorite toy for sure and made you a very happy boy.

FANATIC

JUST 6 SiMPLE RULES

1. Choose an appropriate time out location.
2. Always issue a warning first.
3. The time out period should last for one minute per year of age.
4. When time is up, remind your child why he was sitting and ask them to apologize.
5. **Important: Do not let them have a crayon with them during time out.**
6. If when threatened with time out they willing say ok and run to the chair, you should probably consider an alternate discipline technique or time out location.

UP TO NO GOOD

Great Scrapbook Idea!

Every once in a while, we stumble upon a mistake that turns out to be exactly what our layout needs. Lisa printed her journaling for this layout onto lined paper only because she ran out of plain white paper. Once she held it up to her layout, however, she loved the results! You never know when an "oops" is going to turn into scrapbooking gold!

Lisa Carroll
Asheville, North Carolina

Supplies: Cardstock; die-cut shapes, patterned paper (Bam Pop); letter stickers (EK Success, Making Memories); number sticker (Li'l Davis); sticker accents (7gypsies); conchos (Scrapworks); title letters (Heidi Swapp); decorative punch (Target); corner rounder; pen

IT'S THE LiTTLe

I love these little moment, where you are being so 'zachary'. You have quite a contankerous personaility. You can be cranky, moody

and sometimes down right mean, but you are also sweet and sensitive. Your little imperfetions make life interesting. I love you, zach!

imPERFEctioNS

Great Scrapbook Idea!

One great way to draw extra attention to your photos is to create visual contrast between them. By incorporating both color and black and white photos into this layout, the eye is instantly drawn in, eager to know more about the story. This technique allows you to use the photos you like, even if the colors don't match.

It's the Little Imperfections

Becky Heisler
Waupaca, Wisconsin

Supplies: Patterned paper (CherryArte, Creative Imaginations, Creative Memories, Making Memories); letter stickers (BasicGrey); rub-on accents (American Crafts); transparency (My Mind's Eye); snowflakes (Heidi Swapp); thread

Super Star Bald Boy

Shannon Taylor
Bristol, Tennessee

Supplies: Digital background and paper (Pure Scrapability); stars (Erikia Ghumm); image editing software (Adobe); Basic, Flea Market fonts (Two Peas in a Bucket)

Super Star Bald Boy

I know you absolutely love shaving your head to drive me insane. But I must admit that even with a shiny noggin you still look like you could be a TV star. You just shine from within.

DATE: Fall Photo Shoot - King College - 2005

Mushmallows

Courtney Walsh
Winnebago, Illinois

Supplies: Scalloped cardstock; clip, patterned paper (Making Memories); letter stickers (Doodlebug, Making Memories); ribbon (Offray); pen; Pass the Chex font (Internet download)

Downhill from Here

Nicole Stark
Roy, Utah

Supplies: Patterned paper (BasicGrey, Bo-Bunny, Daisy D's); letter stickers (BasicGrey, Bo-Bunny, Three Bugs in a Rug); chipboard stars (Li'l Davis); buttons (Doodlebug); rhinestones (My Mind's Eye); arrows (Scenic Route); thread; pen

Great Scrapbook Idea!

One simple way to highlight a particular element on your page is to box it in. This can be done easily with stitching, rub ons, even a trusty marker or gel pen. Creating a box keeps the element looking crisp and neat, all the while dressing up the layout in a clean and simple way.

Imagine

Kerry Zerff
Regina, Saskatchewan, Canada

Supplies: Cardstock; stamps (Gelatins); stamping ink; rhinestones (Westrim); colored pencils; corner rounder; thread; pen

Attention Keeper

Becky Novacek
Fremont, Nebraska

Supplies: Cardstock; patterned paper (Anna Griffin, Scenic Route); letter stickers (American Crafts, BasicGrey); journaling accent, photo corners, rub-on letter (Heidi Swapp); ribbon (May Arts); thread; pen

Just one of the advantages of having

"totally nice sweet!"

-Matthew age 4

Totally

Kim Moreno
Tucson, Arizona

Supplies: Cardstock; patterned paper (American Crafts); letter stickers (Li'l Davis); chipboard frame (Magistical Memories); brads; pigment ink; pen

"i got {a plan}"

I Got a Plan

Jennifer S. Gallacher
American Fork, Utah

Supplies: Cardstock; patterned paper (Dèjà Views, Karen Foster); die-cut letters and shapes (Dèjà Views); chipboard letters (Heidi Swapp); quotation stickers (American Crafts); star brads (Making Memories); chipboard accents, decorative tape, rub-on letters (Li'l Davis); SP You've Got Mail font (Scrapsupply)

Great Scrapbook Idea!

Sometimes you want the focus of your layout to be something other than a photo, like a funny saying of your child at a certain age. In this case, punch up your title by mixing and matching a number of embellishments, like chipboard, stickers and brads. When you want to draw extra attention to the title, this will do it, giving the whole layout a more dynamic look!

Monkey

Courtney Walsh
Winnebago, Illinois

Supplies: Patterned paper (Scenic Route); buttons (Autumn Leaves); pigment ink; pen; 2Peas Airplanes font (Two Peas in a Bucket)

the friend we know as
"monkey"

HAND APPETIZER
HAND SANSITIZER
HAND SAPENTIZER
HAND HEPITIZER
HAND SEPENITIZER

HAND SANITIZER - ALEX STYLE

2 WEEK ROAD TRIP JULY 2006

ON THE
ROAD

Hand Sanitizer

Wendy Inman
Virginia Beach, Virginia

Supplies: Cardstock; patterned paper, sticker accents (Karen Foster)

Great Scrapbook Idea!

Allow your layouts to be touched, not just seen! Kellie created this funky, handmade look on her page by cutting random strips of fabric, fraying the edges, and then sewing the strips onto the page while pinching and scrunching them. Consider adding sewing notions or hand stitching to your next layout for that touchable texture fingers can't resist!

Big Boy

Kellie Hayes
Frankston, Victoria, Australia

Supplies: Cardstock; patterned paper (Chatterbox); plastic letters (Heidi Swapp); letter stickers (Doodlebug, Scenic Route); stamps (7gypsies); fabric; thread; pigment ink; pen

School Days

Sarah van Wijck
Avalon Beach, New South Wales, Australia

Supplies: Cardstock; patterned paper (Autumn Leaves, Mustard Moon); letter stickers (American Crafts); chipboard accent (Maya Road); flower (Prima); stamp (7gypsies); stamping ink; brad; corner rounder; pen

Baby or Boy

Deena Wuest
Goessel, Kansas

Supplies: Digital arrows and brushes (Designer Digitals); image editing software (Adobe); Anthology, Avant Garde, Eight Track fonts (Internet download)

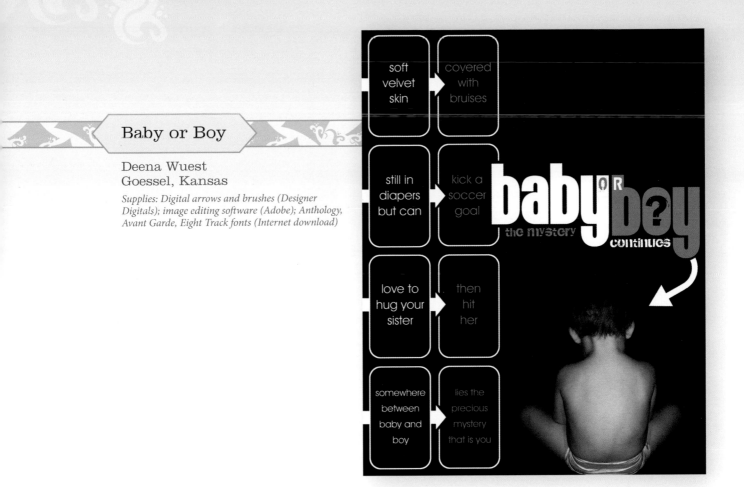

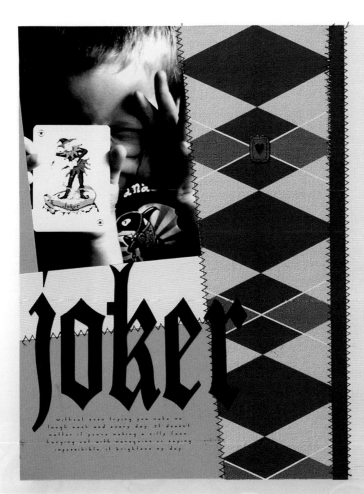

Great Scrapbook Idea!

Certain titles call for an extra large impact. You can easily create an oversized alphabet in a word processing program. Type your text into a new document, enlarge the font size, and then change the style so the letters are outlined. Next, use the program's drawing menu to flip the text horizontally. Print the title on the back of a sheet of patterned paper and cut it out. Voila! An easy high-impact title.

Joker

Kerry Zerff
Regina, Saskatchewan, Canada

Supplies: Cardstock; patterned paper (Imagination Project); charm; thread; 2Peas Think Small font (Two Peas in a Bucket)

Wasn't this photo taken just yesterday? How come it feels like we blinked and you were no longer this chubby-cheeked sweet baby? Someone should have warned us how fast time would go and how even soaking up every moment would still not stop you from growing.

BLINK

Now, you are turning into such a cheerful, wonderful young boy right before my eyes. We are such proud parents! Before we know it, you will be all grown-up. We can't slow time, but we can soak up everything about you from blink to blink.

Blink

Ivette Valladares
Aventura, Florida

Supplies: Cardstock; patterned paper (Fancy Pants); brads, letter stickers (Making Memories); rub-on accents (BasicGrey); flowers (Prima); dye ink; buttons (Bazzill); corner rounder

Superstar Smile

Kimberly Archer
Gainesville, Georgia

Supplies: Cardstock; patterned paper (Die Cuts With A View); die-cut letters (Provo Craft); pen

Good Morning Sunshine

Jill Geraghty-Groves
Springfield, Queensland, Australia

Supplies: Cardstock; patterned paper (BasicGrey, Fancy Pants); letters (Heidi Swapp, We R Memory Keepers); chipboard (Magistical Memories); paint; rub-on accents (SEI); flowers; brads; solvent ink; thread; pen

Girls Love Country Boys

Amy Cutler
Irvona, Pennsylvania

Supplies: Cardstock; patterned paper (Cosmo Cricket, Creative Imaginations, Mustard Moon); chipboard letters and heart (Heidi Swapp); letter stickers (BasicGrey); stamp (Poppy Ink); pigment ink; cardboard; staples; ribbon (unknown); sandpaper; pen

Great Scrapbook Idea!

Be on the lookout for fun alternatives to actual letters to create your next stand-out title. With so many cute embellishments available, you're bound to find a way to use them in your titles! The circles on these pages are not only functional, but decorative as well, and add a creative touch to the pages.

Frog Prince

Kelly Bryan
Avon Lake, Ohio

Supplies: Cardstock; patterned paper (Anna Griffin); letter stickers (American Crafts); chipboard crown (Scenic Route); buttons (Autumn Leaves); rub-on accents (BasicGrey, CherryArte); rhinestone accent (Heidi Swapp); floss

One Interesting Bug

Charity Hassel
Jacksonville, Florida

Supplies: Cardstock; patterned paper (Daisy D's, Scenic Route); chipboard letters (Pressed Petals); plastic letters (Heidi Swapp); letter stickers (Arctic Frog); chipboard accent (KI Memories); brads; ribbon (Rhonna Farrer)

Laugh

Sarah van Wijck
Avalon Beach, New South
Wales, Australia

Supplies: Cardstock; patterned paper (BasicGrey); epoxy and letter stickers (KI Memories); stamps (Greener Pastures); chipboard arrow (Jenni Bowlin); corner rounder; stamping ink

I love this photo...this is you raw
and real. Laughing and giggling while
I try to get you to stand still.
This is my little boy. The one who loves
a cuddle with Mum and a rumble
with Dad. Please don't ever grow up!

laugh

James at 4 LOVES: Sponge Bob, Steak, Shrimp Scampi, worms, gummi bears, anything GUMMI.

Daddy is his FAVORITE person and gets very excited when he gets home from work.

He loves to watch BROTHER BEAR, and falls asleep to it every night.

Favorite word: WHY! Why this, why that. Why do I have to.

James: April 2006

James at 4

Tammi Auayfuay
Surprise, Arizona

Supplies: Cardstock; patterned paper (Rhonna Designs); chipboard letter (BasicGrey); chipboard stars (Making Memories); acrylic paint; brads; pigment ink; rub-on letters and accents (EK Success); circle cutter

Baby Jon

Lisa Hoel
San Jose, California

Supplies: Cardstock; patterned paper (BasicGrey); chipboard letters, letter stamps (Making Memories); acrylic paint; dye, pigment and solvent ink; embossing powder; photo turn (7gypsies); brad; snowflake stamps (Plaid); adhesive foam; pen

Great Scrapbook Idea!

Take the guess-work out of scrapbooking by sticking with a coordinated set of patterned papers and embellishments. Most manufacturers create product lines complete with papers, embellishments and just about everything else you need to create a beautifully coordinated page.

Erick

Shannon Brouwer
Gilbert, Arizona

Supplies: Cardstock; chipboard letters and accents, patterned paper (Scenic Route); corner rounder; CBX Rust font (Two Peas in a Bucket)

That Impish Grin

Crystal Jeffrey Rieger
Woodbridge, Ontario, Canada

Supplies: Cardstock; patterned paper (American Crafts, KI Memories); chipboard letters (Li'l Davis, Making Memories); chipboard accents (Deluxe Designs, Making Memories); clip, snaps (Making Memories); ribbon (Michaels, Wrights); rub-on letters and accents (7gypsies, Making Memories); floral sequins (Westrim); buttons (American Crafts, unknown); acrylic paint; pen

An Intriguing Child

Jill Geraghty-Groves
Springfield, Queensland, Australia

Supplies: Cardstock; patterned paper (BasicGrey, Scenic Route); letter stickers (American Crafts); chipboard leaves (Magistical Memories); stamp (Purple Onion); chipboard (CherryArte); sticker accents (Making Memories); solvent ink; thread

100% Authentic

Sara Wise
Wasilla, Alaska

Supplies: Cardstock; patterned paper (Piggy Tales); chipboard letters, transparent star (Heidi Swapp); stamps (Autumn Leaves, Sassafras Lass); rub-on accents (MaisyMo, Scenic Route); twill accents, wooden number (Li'l Davis); staples; decorative scissors; dye ink; pen

Great Scrapbook Idea!

Looking for a different way to journal your subject's own words? Try interviewing them! Creating a short list of questions and recording the answers will allow you to preserve a person's own unique voice. This works well for documenting anything from a child's favorite things to a grandparent's life story.

Q & A

Ria Mojica
Pasig, Metro Manila, Philippines

Supplies: Patterned paper, rub-on trim (Autumn Leaves); acrylic paint; fibers (FiberScraps); die-cut shapes (Sizzix); stamps (Autumn Leaves, Stampendous); acrylic paint; spiral clip; brads; denim cloth; pen

Great Scrapbook Idea!

Sometimes the tiniest addition to your layout makes the biggest statement. By tying and knotting string to the letters and buttons on this page, Angie was able to create texture and visual interest. What finishing touches can you add to give your page a unique, detailed look?

Sweet Boy

Angie Kajfasz
Port Clinton, Ohio

Supplies: Cardstock; die-cut letters, patterned paper (Crate Paper); floss; buttons (Autumn Leaves); ribbon, tag (unknown); chalk ink; pen

Handsome Devil

Courtney Kelly
Anchorage, Alaska

Supplies: Cardstock; patterned paper (American Crafts, Doodlebug); chipboard letters, letter stickers (KI Memories); transparent stars (Heidi Swapp); brads; staples

On the scrapbook photo:

Just one of those moments caught on film that makes my heart squeeze. Perfection!

PRECIOUS

· 14 months · June 2005 ·

Precious

Crystal Jeffrey Rieger
Woodbridge, Ontario, Canada

Supplies: Cardstock; patterned paper (My Mind's Eye, Paper Adventures); chipboard accent (Grafix); floss; buttons (unknown); flower (Wal-Mart); rub-on letters (Melissa Frances); tag (American Tag); pen

Handsome Dude

Summer Ford
Bulverde, Texas

Supplies: Cardstock; felt accent, patterned paper (Tinkering Ink); chipboard letter (Making Memories); rub-on letters (Me & My Big Ideas); acrylic paint; dye ink; Bookman Old Style font (Microsoft)

On the scrapbook photo:

hanDsome Dude

Hunter, you are growing up to be one handsome little dude! You have definitely transformed over the last year from chubby toddler to a lean and strong little boy. It is amazing to watch you grow and to imagine the man you will become one day.

Ahoy Matey

Jennifer Emch
Lorain, Ohio

Supplies: Cardstock; patterned paper (Autumn Leaves, Making Memories); chipboard letters (EK Success); letter stickers (American Crafts); buttons (Autumn Leaves); chipboard heart (Heidi Swapp); sticker accents (7gypsies); journaling card (Jenni Bowlin); pen

Play with Me

Terri Hayes
Cary, North Carolina

Supplies: Patterned paper (Creative Imaginations, Daisy D's, SEI); letter stickers (Making Memories); sticker accents (Creative Imaginations, My Mind's Eye); chipboard accent (Buzz & Bloom); rub-on accent (7gypsies); ribbon (unknown); pen

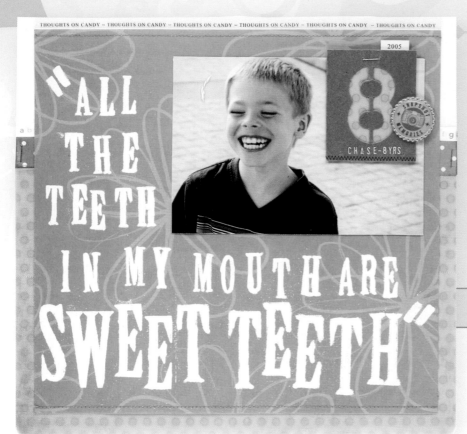

Great Scrapbook Idea!

Sometimes, you have a bit of journaling that needs to stand on its own. Super size your journaling and allow it to serve a dual purpose, acting as both the layout's title and its journaling. You can use large text, foam stamps, chipboard, stickers or a combination of various types of letters. The result will be dynamic and unforgettable!

Sweet Tooth

Mary MacAskill
Calgary, Alberta, Canada

Supplies: Cardstock; patterned paper (BasicGrey, KI Memories); vellum; stamps (Gelatins); embossing powder; letter stencil (Avery); rub-on letters and accents (American Crafts, Autumn Leaves); metal accent (K&Co.); ribbon (American Crafts, Offray); corner rounder; staples

Sweet Jake

Stephanie Hamen
Hoffman Estates, Illinois

Supplies: Cardstock; patterned paper, rub-on words and accents (My Mind's Eye); letter stickers (American Crafts); dye ink; pen

The Boss

Pia Salem-Lopez
Dasmariñas, Cavite, Philippines

*Supplies: Cardstock; patterned paper (BasicGrey);
letter stickers (BasicGrey, unknown); chipboard
accents (We R Memory Keepers, unknown); chipboard
letters (Imagination Project); sticker accent (7gypsies);
pigment ink; buttons; brads; ribbons (unknown); floss;
image editing software (Adobe); pen*

Great Scrapbook Idea!

Adding a patterned border is a
wonderful way to frame your page,
but don't stop there! Try Kelly's
technique of hand stitching a bright
box around the patterned border on
a page. You'll end up with a playful
border that adds dimension and
texture to your layout.

Sweet Boy

Kelly Bryan
Avon Lake, Ohio

*Supplies: Cardstock; patterned paper (My
Mind's Eye, Scenic Route); felt flowers and letters
(American Crafts); die-cut flowers (My Mind's Eye);
brads (Little Black Dress, Making Memories); photo
turns (7gypsies); floss; chalk ink; pen*

Great Scrapbook Idea!

For a simple way of adding visual interest, consider Lisa's technique. Punch a circle out of the empty space on your photo, allowing enough room to hold an embellishment or other element of your design. It's a tiny trick, but just the kind of detail that makes you look twice.

Jordan

Lisa Tutman-Oglesby
Mundelein, Illinois

Supplies: Cardstock; patterned paper (BasicGrey, My Mind's Eye); journaling card, transparency (My Mind's Eye); letter stickers (American Crafts); butterfly (K&Co.); sticker accents (BasicGrey, Pebbles); chipboard accents (Creative Imaginations, Fancy Pants); rub-on words (Fancy Pants); brads; chalk; pen

In These Eyes

Jill Geraghty-Groves
Springfield, Queensland, Australia

Supplies: Cardstock; patterned paper (Dream Street); chipboard letters (Heidi Swapp); ribbon (BasicGrey, Making Memories); beaded wire (Stemma); paint; Diamond Glaze (JudiKins)

Be True to You

Tracy A. Weinzapfel Burgos
Ramona, California

Supplies: Cardstock; patterned paper (Fiber Scraps); rub-on letters (C-Thru); thread; twill (unknown); Prissy Frat Boy font (Internet download)

My Wish

Angie Kajfasz
Port Clinton, Ohio

Supplies: Cardstock; patterned paper (All My Memories); chipboard letters and accents (KI Memories, Scenic Route); brads; ribbon (American Crafts); pen

Great Scrapbook Idea!

We are all familiar with using circles, rectangles and squares on our layouts, but the triangle is often underused. Experiment with this funky shape as Shannon has done in creating this bold layout. When coupled with thick, strong lines and bright, bold colors, the triangle is the perfect shape to take center stage!

Reach

Shannon Taylor
Bristol, Tennessee

Supplies: Cardstock; chipboard letters (Heidi Swapp); ribbon (Offray); brads; buttons (Autumn Leaves, Junkitz); denim pocket; pen

Finally

Annette Pixley
Scappoose, Oregon

Supplies: Cardstock; die-cut shapes, patterned paper (Memories Complete); die-cut letters (Provo Craft); pen

Pure Joy

Kathy Fesmire
Athens, Tennessee

Supplies: Cardstock; patterned paper (BasicGrey, Bo-Bunny, Provo Craft); letter stickers (Sticker Studio); rub-on letters, numbers and stitching (Colorbok, Daisy D's, Paper Studio); bookplates (Queen & Co.); brads; buttons; chalk ink; circle punch; circle cutter

Superstar Quality

Ivette Valladares
Aventura, Florida

Supplies: Cardstock; patterned paper (CherryArte, Scenic Route), letter stickers (Sticker Studio), rhinestone word (Me & My Big Ideas); brads (Junkitz, Making Memories); button; vellum quote (Dèjá Views); bookplate (Daisy D's); ribbon (Bazzill)

climb high, climb far, your goal the sky your aim the star.

superstar

Quality

Master Monkey

Betsy Veldman
Rock Valley, Iowa

Supplies: Cardstock; patterned paper (BasicGrey, Die Cuts With A View, Scenic Route); letter stickers (Die Cuts With A View, Doodlebug); sticker accents (7gypsies, KI Memories); chipboard letter, rub-on word (Scenic Route); brads; ribbon (Die Cuts With A View); paper clip (Junkitz)

determined

WELL DONE!
as opposed to medium rare

and

mission

completed

Mission Completed

Terri Davenport
Toledo, Ohio

Supplies: Digital brushes, stamps and tool kits (Designer Digitals); Wellrock Slab font (Internet download)

** Ham ** Show-off ** Goofy boy ** Goof - off ** Silly dude ** Goober ** Funny face ** Silly Billy ** Ding - Dong ** Schmoo ** Little Turkey ** Gooberooni ** Connor's got a bad case of the "sillies" .... as usual! **

Biking and being goofy at Skyview parkJan 28, 07

Ham on Wheels

Nancy L. Korf
Portland, Oregon

Supplies: Digital kit (Club Scrap); hand-drawn accent and journaling (Wacom); image editing software (Adobe); Doodle Massive Headache, Steelfish fonts (Internet download)

Amanda Walter
Pincher Creek, Alberta, Canada

Supplies: Digital letters, papers, words (Little Dreamer Designs); grunge outline (Jessica Sprague); staples (Pickleberrypop)

Scooter

Wendy Inman
Virginia Beach, Virginia

Supplies: Cardstock; patterned paper, sticker accents (Karen Foster); die-cut stars (QuicKutz); corner rounder; stamping ink; sandpaper

Amy Tara Koeppel
Hobe Sound, Florida

Supplies: Patterned paper (BasicGrey); chipboard letters (Scenic Route); rickrack; brads (Jo-Ann's); woven accents (Me & My Big Ideas); charms (American Traditional)

Team Player?

Annemarie Mackin
Safety Harbor, Florida

Supplies: Cardstock; patterned paper (Scenic Route); letter stickers, star punch (EK Success); die-cut letters and stars (QuicKutz); brads; adhesive foam

Learn to Swim

Greta Hammond
Elkhart, Indiana

Supplies: Cardstock; chipboard letters and shapes, letter stickers, patterned paper (Scenic Route); brads; pen

A New Adventure

Cathy Schellenberg
Steinbach, Manitoba,
Canada

Supplies: Patterned paper, ribbon (SEI); foam letters (Creative Imaginations); brad; notebook paper; sandpaper; staples; pen

Tree Climber

Greta Hammond
Elkhart, Indiana

Supplies: Cardstock; patterned paper (KI Memories); chipboard letters (Heidi Swapp); rub-on trim (FontWerks); brads; dye ink; photo corner (QuicKutz); pen

Climber

Trees are like magnets to little boys. You spot one and it pulls you over.

You immediately scout out all of the well placed limbs for climbing.

You then instantly feel the need to climb up in it and see how far you can go.

Never mind the danger. Never mind your attire. Just go, without really thinking about it.

This is definitely a boy thing. And you are definitely a boy.

And He's Off

Megan Thurman
Houston, Texas

Supplies: Chipboard accents, patterned paper (Scenic Route); letter stickers (American Crafts); rhinestones (Heidi Swapp); photo turn (7gypsies); ribbon; stamping ink; corner rounder; sandpaper; pen

August 2006. Connor's first day of preschool. I can't believe my firstborn is old enough for school. Where has the time gone? But he's off. He's on his way. He's got adventures, fun, and learning ahead!

and he's off...

Leaf Blower Boy

Catherine Feegel-Erhardt
Tampa, Florida

Supplies: Cardstock; patterned paper (A2Z, Bo-Bunny); chipboard letters (cut freehand by artist); letter stickers (Making Memories); acrylic paint; stamping ink; adhesive foam; pen

Biker Boy

Peggy Severins
Raamsdonksveer, Noord-Brabant, The Netherlands

Supplies: Cardstock; patterned paper (Urban Lily); metal letters and number (KI Memories); paper frills (Doodlebug); die-cut shapes (Provo Craft, Sizzix); photo anchors, tags (Making Memories); brads; paper piercer; staples

New Dirt Bike

Rebekah Robinson
Shelocta, Pennsylvania

Supplies: Cardstock; patterned paper (A2Z); die-cut letters and shapes (Provo Craft); charm (Imaginisce); hole punch

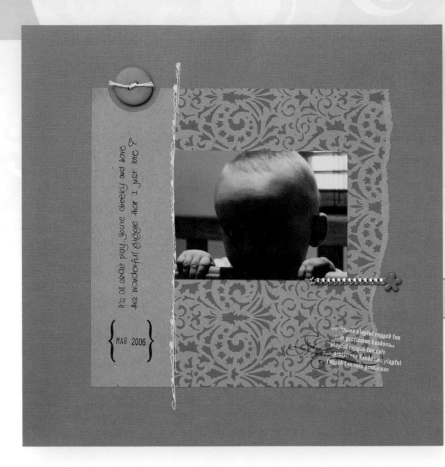

March 2006

Sarah van Wijck
Avalon Beach, New South Wales,
Australia

*Supplies: Cardstock; patterned paper (Making Memories);
rub-on accents (BasicGrey, My Mind's Eye); stamp (7gypsies);
brads; charm; button; string; pen*

Nathan's to Do List

Dana Forti
Claremont, California

*Supplies: Cardstock; patterned paper (Provo Craft); letter stickers (Creative Memories,
Mrs. Grossman's); number stickers (Creative Memories, EK Success, unknown); die-cut
accents (Creative Memories, Die Cuts With A View); paper clips; notebook paper; pen*

brave adventurous courageous brave adventurous

IS that fun?

no fear

adventure

Connor has always been on the cautious side when it comes to trying new things. So imagine my surprise when he boldly went on the 20 foot slide at the carnival. And despite how these photos look, he actually loved this ride. He would squeal with delight at the end and race back to the top. He is such a delight!

Great Scrapbook Idea!

You just never know when inspiration is going to strike! For Megan, this design came together after seeing the opener for a television show. If you keep your eyes open, you'll find inspiration on TV, in magazines, in department stores. Everywhere you look, there's something, even the tiniest detail, that can be translated onto a scrapbook page.

Is That Fun?

Megan Thurman
Houston, Texas

Supplies: Cardstock; chipboard accents, patterned paper (Scenic Route); letter stickers (Doodlebug); rhinestones, star accents (Heidi Swapp); stamping ink; pen

Slow pokes, beware! 'Cause it's only

free way speeds

around here! And if you can't keep up, then be prepared for the consequences. I'm rough. I'm tough. And I'm getting faster everyday. And brakes? Well, these wheels don't need 'em. I'm the driver. I'm the navigator. And if you're crazy enough to cross my path, be prepared to get squished. Of course, I will apologize with my sweetest "I'm sorry." But then it's back to business as usual: tearing down the sidewalk at breakneck speeds, taking curves and corners with just two wheels. And that's just the way I like it!

Freeway Speeds

Jennifer S. Gallacher
American Fork, Utah

Supplies: Cardstock; patterned paper (Karen Foster); letter stickers (Creative Imaginations, Pebbles); photo corners (Creative Imaginations); corner rounder; circle punch; pen; SP You've Got Mail font (Scrapsupply)

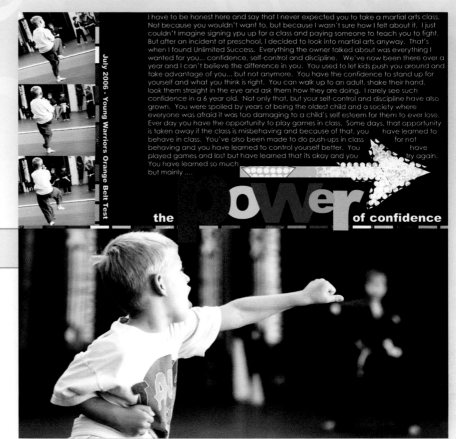

I have to be honest here and say that I never expected you to take a martial arts class. Not because you wouldn't want to, but because I wasn't sure how I felt about it. I just couldn't imagine signing you up for a class and paying someone to teach you to fight. But after an incident at preschool, I decided to look into martial arts anyway. That's when I found Unlimited Success. Everything the owner talked about was everything I wanted for you... confidence, self-control and discipline. We've now been there over a year and I can't believe the difference in you. You used to let kids push you around and take advantage of you... but not anymore. You have the confidence to stand up for yourself and what you think is right. You can walk up to an adult, shake their hand, look them straight in the eye and ask them how they are doing. I rarely see such confidence in a 6 year old. Not only that, but your self-control and discipline have also grown. You were spoiled by years of being the oldest child and a society where everyone was afraid it was too damaging to a child's self esteem for them to ever lose. Ever day you have the opportunity to play games in class. Some days, that opportunity is taken away if the class is misbehaving and because of that, you have learned to behave in class. You've also been made to do push-ups in class for not behaving and you have learned to control yourself better. You have played games and lost but have learned that its okay and you try again. You have learned so much but mainly ....

July 2006 - Young Warriors Orange Belt Test

the **power** of confidence

The Power of Confidence

Tracie Radtke
Chicago, Illinois

Supplies: Digital paper and accents (FishScraps); image editing software (Adobe); Arial Black, Century Gothic fonts (Microsoft)

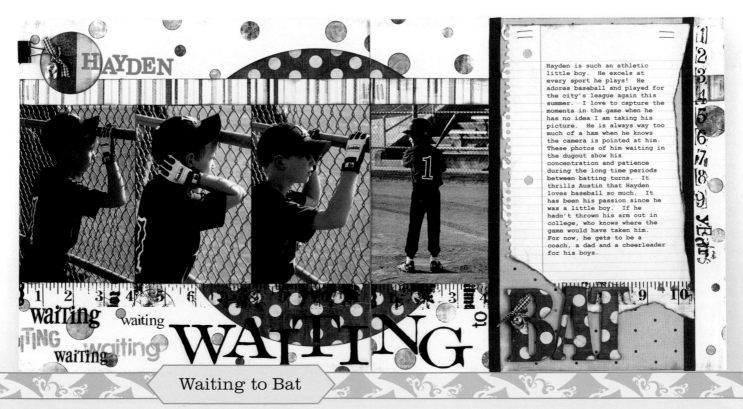

HAYDEN

Hayden is such an athletic little boy. He excels at every sport he plays! He adores baseball and played for the city's league again this summer. I love to capture the moments in the game when he has no idea I am taking his picture. He is always way too much of a ham when he knows the camera is pointed at him. These photos of him waiting in the dugout show his concentration and patience during the long time periods between batting turns. It thrills Austin that Hayden loves baseball so much. It has been his passion since he was a little boy. If he hadn't thrown his arm out in college, who knows where the game would have taken him. For now, he gets to be a coach, a dad and a cheerleader for his boys.

WAITING to BAT

waiting

Waiting to Bat

Kathy Fesmire
Athens, Tennessee

Supplies: Patterned paper (My Mind's Eye); rub-on letters (Colorbok, EK Success, Me & My Big Ideas, Paper Studio); letter stickers (Karen Foster, Wordsworth); rub-on accents (Dee's Designs); chipboard letters (EK Success); charms (Watch Us); ribbons (Offray); circle cutter; binder clip; notebook paper; stamping ink; staples

BRING IT...

{PLAY}
{INSPIRE}
{GROW}
{BELIEVE}
{GIVE}
{REMEMBER}

You take pitching on your Baseball team very seriously. I've heard that some players have to "get in the game" before it even starts. You're definitely one of those players. I realize when I see you before the game begins, off on your own in the field, that you're not trying to separate yourself from your teammates. You are mentally preparing yourself to pitch your best game, and when you say "Bring It ....I hope the other team understands that you mean it.

Bring It

Collette Osuna
Eastpointe, Michigan

Supplies: Cardstock; patterned papers, round stickers, rub-on letters (Sweetwater); brads

Great Scrapbook Idea!

Masculinity is sometimes difficult to convey, but Keitha has found a cool way to do just that! For her background, she first layered masking tape over a sheet of cardstock. Next, she painted the tape cream and then rubbed the entire surface with a paper towel soaked in walnut ink. The result is a leathery looking backdrop for a very masculine page!

Unforgettable QB

Keitha K. Fish
Liberty Township, Ohio

Supplies: Chipboard, patterned paper (AdornIt); chipboard letters (Pressed Petals); chipboard accents (BasicGrey, Li'l Davis); tag (My Mind's Eye); ribbon (Creative Impressions); football accents (Magic Scraps); acrylic paint; brads; masking tape; staples; stamping ink; pen

Little Fan

Rachel Davis
Findlay, Ohio

Supplies: Cardstock; patterned paper (Scenic Route); chipboard letters and stars (American Crafts, Bazzill); rub-on letters (Doodlebug); ink; notebook paper; pen

United Center

Donna Leslie
Tinley Park, Illinois

Supplies: Cardstock; patterned paper (BasicGrey, Frances Meyer, Imagination Project); chipboard stars (Imagination Project); eyelets; thread

St. Louis Cardinals

Kathy Fesmire
Athens, Tennessee

Supplies: Cardstock; patterned paper (Karen Foster); letter stickers (American Crafts, EK Success, K&Co.); tags (Li'l Davis); fabric brads (Paper Studio); bottle cap (EK Success); ribbon (Offray); chalk ink; pen

Hockey Dreams

Jennifer Backler
Burlington, Ontario, Canada

Supplies: Cardstock; patterned paper (Scrapworks); letter stickers (Sticker Studio); rub-on letters (American Crafts); metal letter (Jo-Ann's); brads (Bazzill, Findings & Things, Heidi Swapp, Queen & Co.); chipboard accents (Bazzill, Heidi Swapp); thread; stamps (Gelatins); stamping ink; ribbon (unknown); pen

Great Scrapbook Idea!

Boys are always on the move, so it's natural to want your pages to communicate that same movement. Allow a trail of carefully placed embellishments to guide the eye around the layout. The result? A dynamic page that will move you.

Learning 2 Score

Greta Hammond
Elkhart, Indiana

Supplies: Cardstock; chipboard letters and photo corners, patterned paper (Scenic Route); sticker accents (American Crafts, Scenic Route); brads; rub-on letters (Making Memories); digital frames (Two Peas in a Bucket); adhesive foam

You Rock

Catherine Feegel-Erhardt
Tampa, Florida

Supplies: Cardstock; patterned paper (A2Z); letters (outline of Heidi Swapp letters); stamping ink; sandpaper; pen

Just Hosing Around

Suzy Plantamura
Laguna Niguel, California

Supplies: Cardstock; patterned paper (Chatterbox, K&Co.); rub-on letters (Me & My Big Ideas); rub-on stitches (We R Memory Keepers); stamping ink; corner rounder; pen

Stand Alone

Jill Jackson-Mills
Roswell, Georgia

Supplies: Cardstock; patterned paper (Scrapworks, unknown); patterned transparency (Magic Scraps); letter stickers (Provo Craft); sticker accent (Karen Russell)

Great Scrapbook Idea!

It's never easy when your family faces hardship, but there's no better time to utilize your scrapbooking as a source of strength and encouragement. On this layout, Jennifer was able to capture her emotion and pride for her son who had been recently diagnosed with cancer. Because she wrote it down, her family will never wonder how she felt during this difficult time.

Fight with All You've Got

Jennifer S. Gallacher
American Fork, Utah

Supplies: Cardstock; patterned paper (Karen Foster, Li'l Davis, MOD); chipboard bookplate, ribbon (Li'l Davis); stamp (Stampendous); watermark ink; eyelets; circle punch; rub-on phrase (Dèjà Views); Century Gothic font (Microsoft); Quigley Wiggley title font (ScrapVillage)

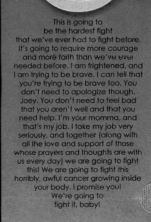

This is going to be the hardest fight that we've ever had to fight before. It's going to require more courage and more faith than we've ever needed before. I am frightened, and I am trying to be brave. I can tell that you're trying to be brave too. You don't need to apologize though, Joey. You don't need to feel bad that you aren't well and that you need help. I'm your momma, and that's my job. I take my job very seriously, and together (along with all the love and support of those whose prayers and thoughts are with us every day) we are going to fight this! We are going to fight this horribly, awful cancer growing inside your body. I promise you! We're going to fight it, baby!

Good to the Last Drop

Suzy Plantamura
Laguna Niguel, California

Supplies: Cardstock; patterned paper (Karen Foster, NRN Design); chipboard letters (American Crafts); chipboard arrow (unknown); stamping ink; corner rounder; pen

Will @ 19

Shelley May
North Syracuse, New York

Supplies: Cardstock; chipboard letters, patterned paper (Bisous); metal accents (Making Memories); rhinestones (Heidi Swapp); crimper (Fiskars); dye ink; pen

Great Scrapbook Idea!

It's no secret that boys aren't made of sugar and spice, so you have to be ready to scrap the mud, the dirt and yes, even the black eyes! You might find yourself cringing to think about bruises, broken bones and silly accidents your son gets himself into, but remember, it's what makes him a boy. Scrap it!

Shine On

Shaunte Wadley
Lehi, Utah

Supplies: Cardstock; patterned paper (Making Memories); die-cut letters and brackets (Provo Craft); transparency (Rusty Pickle); thread; Harting font (Dafont)

What If

Jill Jackson-Mills
Roswell, Georgia

Supplies: Cardstock; fibers, patterned paper (BasicGrey); labels (Dymo); file folder (Old Navy); chipboard letters (unknown)

Great Scrapbook Idea!

Don't let the blank journaling block intimidate you! Next time your stumped for words, simply start talking and record what you say— exactly as you say it. Writing doesn't have to be a throwback to English 101, just concentrate on keeping it real. This way, you're sure to allow your true voice to shine through.

Freshman

Jill Jackson-Mills
Roswell, Georgia

Supplies: Cardstock; brad, patterned paper (unknown); plastic letters (Heidi Swapp, Jo-Ann's); rub-on numbers (BasicGrey); ribbon (Offray); staple

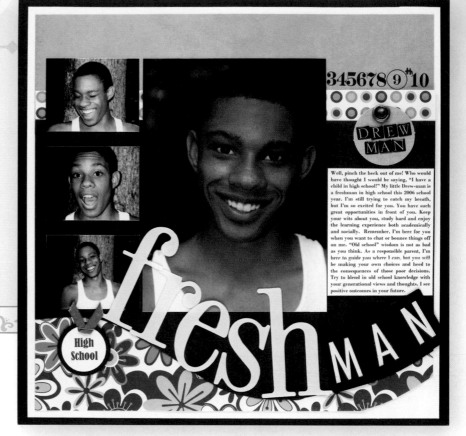

Well, pinch the heck out of me! Who would have thought I would be saying, "I have a child in high school!" My little Drew-man is a freshman in high school this 2006 school year. I'm still trying to catch my breath, but I'm so excited for you. You have such great opportunities in front of you. Keep your wits about you, study hard and enjoy the learning experience both academically and socially. Remember, I'm here for you when you want to chat or bounce things off on me. "Old school" wisdom is not as bad as you think. As a responsible parent, I'm here to guide you where I can, but you will be making your own choices and heed to the consequences of those poor decisions. Try to blend in old school knowledge with your generational views and thoughts. I see positive outcomes in your future.

austin · age 10

.....the list.................

new skate shoes

ipod shuffle

football games

The A List

Katrina Simeck
Colchester, Vermont

Supplies: Cardstock; patterned paper, rub-on letters (One Heart One Mind); chipboard letters (Pressed Petals); chipboard circles (SEI); pen

Great Scrapbook Idea!

As your kids get older, one thing they won't want you to do is put words into their mouths! Make sure to include your older children's voices on pages about them. This will make the layouts more personal and more special to them as the years go by!

Things U Love

Mimi Leinbach
Reading, Pennsylvania

Supplies: Cardstock; patterned paper (Creative Imaginations, Three Bugs in a Rug); chipboard letter, die-cut shapes (Three Bugs in a Rug); stamps (Technique Tuesday); dye ink; embossing enamel; ribbon (Michaels); pen

Imagine-Ation

Lisa Cloud
Sioux City, Iowa

Supplies: Patterned paper (Bam Pop); transparent letters (Heidi Swapp); rub-on accents (BasicGrey, Making Memories); transparencies (Autumn Leaves, Hambly); chipboard accents (Imagination Project); photo turns (7gypsies); brads; acrylic paint; staples; pen

chapter

Open Heart

We all have memories that tug at our heartstrings—those
moments that make us smile or cry, or make our hearts
skip a beat. It's our relationships that create
these moments in our lives. But often, we
struggle to find the right way to express
our emotions. We fear being too sappy
or insincere. Instead of allowing this
struggle to scare you into leaving
these precious memories out your
scrapbooks, use this chapter to
discover ways to effectively document
those people closest to your heart.
From spouses and grandparents to
special friends we will never
forget, this chapter covers all
the relationships that make
us who we are.

Nine

Amy Peterman
Muskegon, Michigan

*Supplies: Cardstock; patterned paper
(My Mind's Eye); tissue paper; letter
and number stickers (All My Memories,
Creative Imaginations, EK Success); stamps,
transparency (Creative Imaginations);
acrylic paint; rub-on accents (BasicGrey);
buttons (vintage); staples; pen*

Great Scrapbook Idea!

Feeling boxed in by the straight lines
that confine your scrapbook pages?
Break out of the box with a heart-
shaped or circular layout. You'll spark
new ideas as the boundaries of your
page change! Specially shaped pages
slip easily into a page protector, but they
make great display art as well.

Sweet Stolen Moments

Grace Castillo
Anaheim, California

*Supplies: Scalloped cardstock (Bazzill); epoxy stickers,
patterned paper, ribbon, transparency (Creative
Imaginations); die-cut shapes, letter stickers
(KI Memories); pen*

Loving U

Paola López-Araiza Osante
Mexico City, Mexico

Supplies: Patterned paper (Cosmo Cricket, KI Memories, Rusty Pickle); index tabs, transparent letters (Heidi Swapp); chipboard heart (Imagination Project); floss; rub-on quotes (7gypsies); twill (Hot Off The Press); dye ink; thread

Great Scrapbook Idea!

For a funky look, try using index tabs as a makeshift frame for a focal point photo. Tabs also make great borders for journaling or even an entire page. With this simple twist, you'll add color, visual interest and the perfect decorative touch for a layout that's beyond the ordinary.

Love Forever

Cricket Rawlins
Lake Villa, Illinois

Supplies: Cardstock; buttons, patterned paper (Autumn Leaves); chipboard letters (Heidi Swapp); acrylic paint; flowers (Michaels); stamp (Stampin' Up); solvent ink; label holder (7gypsies); brads; ribbon; floss; corner rounder; pen

Kiss

April Foster
Bowling Green, Kentucky

Supplies: Cardstock; patterned paper (My Mind's Eye, Sassafras Lass); decorative tape, clock accent, letters (Heidi Swapp); pen

6.5 Years

Michelle Cathcart
Sugar Grove, Pennsylvania

Supplies: Cardstock; patterned paper (SEI); chipboard accents (Maya Road); letter and number stickers, rhinestone brads (Making Memories); rub-on accents (American Crafts); transparency (Hambly); flowers (Prima); photo turns (Jo-Ann's); dimensional paint

Great Scrapbook Idea!

Looking for a quick and easy solution for adding frames to your photos? For an easy photo mat that is as cheap as it is simple, just sand the edges of your photo with sandpaper. This distressed look is a great way to add an instant photo frame without going to a lot of trouble!

I Heart You

Staci Compher
Carleton, Michigan

Supplies: Patterned paper (Scenic Route); chipboard letters (American Crafts, Chatterbox); chipboard accent (Making Memories); die-cut shapes (Sassafras Lass, Scenic Route); rub-on accents (BasicGrey); stamps (Close to My Heart); stamping ink; pen

Dream

Jill Cornell
Windsor Heights, Iowa

Supplies: Cardstock; die-cut shapes and words, patterned paper and transparency (My Mind's Eye); brads; ribbon (May Arts); sandpaper; pen

Great Scrapbook Idea!

If you're feeling artistic, you might want to try your hand at some doodling. Anything goes in the world of doodles, so get out that trusty pen and make a masterpiece! Experiment with different colored pens and markers or just stick to one color; either way, you're free to be creative.

Love

Catherine Feegel-Erhardt
Tampa, Florida

Supplies: Cardstock; patterned paper (Bo-Bunny); rub-on letters (EK Success); stamping ink; corner rounder; pen

Happily Ever After

Sara Wise
Wasilla, Alaska

Supplies: Cardstock; patterned paper (Junkitz); ribbon (May Arts); ribbon slides (Pebbles); rub-on accents (MaisyMo); rub-on words (Making Memories); dye ink; die-cut heart (Provo Craft); pen

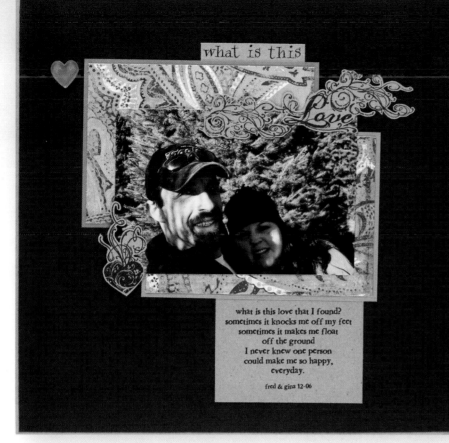

What is This Love?

Gina Pastore
Montague, New Jersey

Supplies: Kraft cardstock; cardstock; patterned paper (My Mind's Eye); rub-on accents (Reminisce); watermark ink; embossing powder; stamps (Inkadinkado); plastic heart (KI Memories); CK Fraternity font (Internet download)

Great Scrapbook Idea!

The next time you need an inventive and inexpensive way to add color to a layout, look no further than your local home improvement store. By stocking up on paint chips you can create a dynamic design that complements your layout. Use paint chips under photos as mats, use them just as they are or cut them in pieces for a mosaic of color to suit any mood.

I & P

Paola López-Araiza Osante
Mexico City, Mexico

Supplies: Paint chips (Dutch Boy); letters (Doodlebug); vellum

The Evans

Angela Ploegman
Bettendorf, Iowa

Supplies: Cardstock; journaling tag, patterned paper, quote accent (My Mind's Eye); chipboard letters (BasicGrey); die-cut letters and shapes (Junkitz, My Mind's Eye); brad; acrylic paint; twill (unknown); decorative punches; chalk ink; pen

Selfless Service

Kelly O'Dell
Cincinnati, Ohio

Supplies: Patterned paper (Karen Foster); digital printed elements (artist's own design); army accents (unknown)

Great Scrapbook Idea!

Leave a piece of history in your scrapbooks by incorporating everyday memorabilia. Anything from dated ticket stubs to grocery receipts to bank machine statements serve as a great way to document your life. Just think how precious these bits of ephemera will be to future generations.

Date

Kelly Fowler
Edmonton, Alberta, Canada

Supplies: Cardstock; patterned paper (KI Memories, My Mind's Eye, Urban Lily); acrylic paint; rickrack; staples; flower token (Doodlebug); wager sheet (Knock Knock); bus transfer stub; pen

Feels Like Home

Amy Elkins
Washougal, Washington

Supplies: Cardstock; frames, patterned paper, tags (Crate Paper); rub-on letters (Autumn Leaves); flower (Making Memories); die-cut shapes (QuicKutz); stamping ink; brad; thread; Bradley Hand ITC font (Internet download)

1940's When my grandmother died in 2004, my family found an amazing stash of photographs in her apartment. For days we flipped through her albums and enjoyed seeing her in her younger years. Two years later, I asked my mother if I could borrow one of the albums so that I could scan the pictures onto my computer to have a digital copy. My first motive in this was so that I would have a digital copy just in case something happened to the originals. My second motive was to scrapbook them. Looking over them again astonishes me! I can't believe that these photographs (taken in 1948 and 1949) are in such good condition! They have been very well taken care of. My favorite thing about these photographs is how happy my grandmother looks as she looks at my grandfather. They were very much in love. In every photograph, she is staring at her prince with eyes of admiration and love. This reminds me of a recent memory. In 1999, my grandfather passed away. I was sitting near my grandmother at the viewing and heard her quietly and with sadness say to herself, "What am I going to do now?" It broke my heart. It still breaks my heart to think about it. She had lost her prince and was lost herself. I didn't fully understand her loss at the time. But now, after seeing these photographs... I understand.

In Love with You

Amy Hummel
St. George, Utah

Supplies: Cardstock; rub-on letters (American Crafts, Heidi Swapp); chipboard shape (Heidi Swapp); paint pen

Great Scrapbook Idea!

To create an interesting design element, Amy used a white permanent marker to carefully fill in the point where her rub-on letters overlap the black line at the top of her page. It's a simple detail, but it creates a striking contrast, and you can't help but give the title a second glance.

Only with You

Kimberly Archer
Gainesville, Georgia

Supplies: Cardstock; patterned paper (K&Co.); chipboard letters (Paper Studio); photo corners (Making Memories); hinge accent, tissue paper (7gypsies); ribbon (unknown); sandpaper; pen; Internet font (Internet download)

Cute Couple

Michelle Cathcart
Sugar Grove, Pennsylvania

Supplies: Cardstock; patterned paper (BasicGrey); chipboard letters, ribbon (unknown); brads; stamping ink; pen

A gentle love, a tender love, a passionate love with BIG plans, and everyday love with quiet moments, a love born of trust and faith. forever ♡

Say Cheese

Eileen Aber
Cincinnati, Ohio

Supplies: Patterned paper (SEI); letter stickers (Polar Bear Press); envelope (Waste Not); photo corners; journaling accent (7gypsies); brads; rub-on accents (American Crafts); circle punch; pen

MAY · 2004

MARCH · 2005

SEPT · 2006

It's one of our favorite things to do... every time we go somewhere new (or old for that matter) we love to hunt down a photo booth.

It's our fun little way of capturing the memories.

say cheese

open

THE LOOK

I like to call it the "A" factor! you + me = amazing. which means Adam + Amber = A-mazing. In some quirky way, I absolutely adore the fact that our names both start with "A" - because it is so cool to scrapbook! This page has been on the backburner of my mind for somehow but after our spontaneous photo shoot on Valentine's Day, I decided I had finally captured our "A" factor style. you, my love, are a mix of ... bomb-silliness, & am a lit-tle taken aback by your wonderful- ... ess, I love that you take the always time to play with me, talk to me, & give me good advice. I love that you give me eskimo kisses. And butterfly kisses. (And yes, even BIG GIRL kisses, haha!) I love that you made me an incredible homemade Valentine card - and that you bought me that crazy-cool plaque that says..."I kiss better than I cook" you know me so well. Most of all, I love that you love God with such passion and zeal and that you love me, quite in spite of myself. you are what makes the "A" factor so incredible! I love you! ♡ Amber

The factor

The "A" Factor

Amber Benton
Panama City, Florida

Supplies: Cardstock; patterned paper (unknown); chipboard heart (Making Memories); letter stickers (Colorbok, Creative Imaginations, Die Cuts With A View, EK Success, Heidi Swapp, Jo-Ann's, K&Co., Making Memories, Me & My Big Ideas, SEI, Wal-Mart); rub-on accents (American Crafts, Heidi Swapp); ribbon, transparent letter (Heidi Swapp); pen

Great Scrapbook Idea!

If you're looking for an easy way to make a statement on your next page, consider repetition. Repeating a design element, a bit of journaling or a series of letters or numbers is a quick and easy way to make your layout cohesive and well designed. It's a simple tried and true rule that works every time!

Make LOVE not war

World of Warcraft

LOVE YA!

World of Warcraft

Ronee Parsons
Olympia, Washington

Supplies: Digital background (Digi Shoppe); patterned paper (Sweet Shoppe Designs); edges, graffiti, grommets, stitches and tears (CatScrap)

Reason 76 Why I Love My Husband

Terri Hayes
Cary, North Carolina

Supplies: Cardstock; patterned paper (Fancy Pants, My Mind's Eye, Scenic Route); letter stickers (American Crafts); rub-on accents (Fancy Pants); chipboard accents (Scenic Route); buttons (unknown); pen

Great Scrapbook Idea!

For a different take on journaling, why not flip it on its side? Your reader won't mind turning the page, and it adds a cool design element to the layout. Use your own handwriting, journaling strips or a block of solid text—all would work just as well (and be a bit more interesting!) turned on their side.

I Married an Axe Murderer

Crystal Jeffrey Rieger
Woodbridge, Ontario, Canada

Supplies: Patterned paper (K&Co.); letter stamps (Technique Tuesday); letter stickers (EK Success); chipboard letters (Li'l Davis); chipboard accents (Heidi Swapp, MOD); acrylic paint; clips (Making Memories); solvent ink; ribbon (Michaels); rub-on accents (7gypsies); sandpaper; staples; tags (Avery); pen

Porter

Michelle Coleman
Layton, Utah

*Supplies: Digital elements
(Little Dreamer Designs)*

Sweet Things in Life

Charity Hassel
Jacksonville, Florida

*Supplies: Chipboard accents, journaling
accents, patterned paper (Cosmo Cricket);
button brads (Karen Foster); pen*

Lucky

Chrys Queen Rose
Tracy, California

Supplies: Cardstock; chipboard letters and accents, patterned paper (Scenic Route); rhinestone; thread

You must know that I feel like the luckiest mom in the world to have a wonderful little boy like you to call my own.

My *Beautiful* girls

Motherhood is a wild ride.
And it seems that on most days I simply cannot hold on tight enough.. My heart breaks a thousand times when I see you two struggling with the same issues I had growing up.. I know how difficult it is, just being a girl and staying strong and true to yourself. Many times I just want to reach out and make everything better, easier.. But I also know that my own personal struggles are what have made me strong. And given me the courage to reach for my dreams. So, I share with you all that I know, all that I have learned, and when the time is right I will let you go. And while there is no way of knowing where you will end up. I will always be here, your safe place throughout your journey..

10.29.06

My Beautiful Girls

Michelle Coleman
Layton, Utah

Supplies: Digital embellishments, papers and stamps (Little Dreamer Designs)

Together We Are One

Kim Moreno
Tucson, Arizona

Supplies: Cardstock; letter stickers, patterned paper (Chatterbox); brads; chipboard (Magistical Memories); pigment ink; floss; transparency; pen

4 of a Kind

Grace Castillo
Anaheim, California

Supplies: Cardstock; patterned paper (7gypsies, Imagination Project); chipboard accents (Imagination Project); letter stickers (American Crafts); rub-on letters (Making Memories); pen

Great Scrapbook Idea!

A look that's both shabby and chic is instantly noticeable and often coveted in the world of scrapbooking. One quick and easy way to obtain this look on your layouts is to add just a few wisps of paint along the edges of the page. This creates the romantic, worn feel that every shabby but chic layout calls for!

Wait

Theresa C. Tyree
Sullivan, Missouri

Supplies: Cardstock; chipboard accents, eyelet ribbon, patterned paper (Making Memories); chipboard letters (Heidi Swapp); acrylic paint; pins (Heidi Grace); pen

I Heart Them

Katrina Huerta
Glendale, Arizona

Supplies: Patterned paper (Dream Street); chipboard letters, journaling accent (Heidi Swapp); chipboard heart (Magistical Memories); stamp (Autumn Leaves); pigment ink; flowers (Bazzill, Heidi Swapp); button (Autumn Leaves); rickrack; pen

Great Scrapbook Idea!

You love the way ledger paper looks on your layouts, but did you know it's functional too? The lines provide instant guides for you to line up journaling, titles, photos and other page elements in a snap! Look for ways you can save yourself time by making use of what's already part of your layout!

I Asked God for a Miracle, and He Gave Me 4

Alicia Giess
Mansfield, Ohio

Supplies: Cardstock; patterned paper (Mustard Moon, Scenic Route); chipboard number, letter stickers (BasicGrey); chipboard letters (Scenic Route); stamps (American Crafts); brads; adhesive foam; pen

Revolve

Deena Wuest
Goessel, Kansas

Supplies: Digital paper, shapes, and stamps (Designer Digitals); image editing software (Adobe); Avant Garde font (Internet download)

Wild Thing

Michelle Engel
Brantford, Ontario, Canada

Supplies: Cardstock; patterned paper (Pink Martini); overlay (Hambly); chipboard letters (Maya Road); embossing powders (Gelatins); stamping ink; brads (Making Memories); foam flowers (Dollarstore); epoxy circles (unknown); pen

They Just Need Love

Holly Pitroff
Mooresville, North Carolina

Supplies: Patterned paper (My Mind's Eye); chipboard accent (BasicGrey); letter stickers, rub-on word (Making Memories); chipboard frame (Junkitz); ribbon (May Arts); rub-on letters (Creative Imaginations, Heidi Swapp); dye ink; adhesive foam; twine; Tempus Sans font (Internet download)

Great Scrapbook Idea!

Decorative page elements are everywhere, and you don't have to go far to get them on your layouts! Cute little birds and animals can easily be added to your pages with the simple sketch of your hand. Just draw your own design onto a piece of patterned paper and cut it out. You can add detail with your pen or just let the paper's pattern draw the attention.

I Heart U Forever

Cathy Pascual
Bellevue, Washington

Supplies: Cardstock; patterned paper (BasicGrey, Creative Imaginations, Daisy D's, K&Co., Scrapworks); die-cut letters (Daisy D's); rub-on accents (BasicGrey, Die Cuts With A View); tabs (7gypsies); dye ink; decorative scissors; ribbon (Beaux Regards); staples; thread; pen; digital frame (Digital Design Essentials)

A Heart Complete

Cathy Schellenberg
Steinbach, Manitoba, Canada

Supplies: Cardstock; scalloped cardstock (Bazzill); patterned paper (Autumn Leaves); transparent letters (Heidi Swapp); chipboard accents (Maya Road); brads; flowers (Prima); stamps (Autumn Leaves); stamping ink; rub-on letters (Making Memories); photo corners; glitter; pen; DiMurphic font (Internet download)

Great Scrapbook Idea!

Don't wait for *The New York Times* to finish a crossword puzzle! For a clever way to create a title or to journal, place letter stickers or rub-ons that complement your page design in the empty puzzle boxes. The end result will be undeniably adorable.

I Love My Kids with All My Heart

Alicia Giess
Mansfield, Ohio

Supplies: Cardstock; patterned paper (KI Memories, Mustard Moon); letter and accent stickers (American Crafts); fabric paint; heart ribbon (May Arts); stamping ink; pen

Adore You

Missy Neal
Campbell, California

Supplies: Chipboard letters and accents, patterned paper (Fancy Pants); flowers (Prima); stamp (Li'l Davis); buttons; pen

Little Love

Caroline Langlois
Vancouver, British Columbia, Canada

Supplies: Cardstock; patterned paper (BasicGrey); letter stickers (Making Memories); brads (American Crafts, Making Memories, Queen & Co.); spiral clip; ribbon (American Craft); flowers (Prima); acrylic paint; glitter glue; rhinestones; chipboard; pen

Great Scrapbook Idea!

Looking for a way to do your part for the environment? Recycle what you can, turning non-traditional items into scrapbooking art! On this layout, Cindy used a mesh produce bag as an integral part of her design. What can you find lying around your house that would make an inexpensive and brilliant addition to your next layout?

You Shine

Cindy Tobey
Kentwood, Michigan

Supplies: Chipboard letters and shapes, patterned paper (Fancy Pants); paper frills (Doodlebug); acrylic paint; pigment ink; buttons (Autumn Leaves, unknown); felt; floss; pipe cleaner; mesh produce bag; staples; pen; AL Uncle Charles font (Two Peas in a Bucket)

My Everything

Angela J. Prieto
Stockton, Kansas

Supplies: Patterned paper (We R Memory Keepers); chipboard letters (Heidi Swapp); chipboard flowers (Pressed Petals); rub-on letters (Making Memories); rub-on accents (Die Cuts With A View, Three Bugs in a Rug); pigment ink; acrylic paint; pen

I Love Thee

Yvette Adams
Banks, Australian Capital Territory, Australia

Supplies: Patterned paper (BasicGrey); chipboard circle, rub-on letters (Heidi Swapp, unknown); paper flower (Fancy Pants); brad; tags; beads; jewelry pin; fabric flower (unknown); thread; 2Peas Billboard, Ancient Script fonts (Internet download)

Lovely

Lisa Kisch
Ottawa, Ontario, Canada

Supplies: Cardstock; patterned paper (KI Memories); letter stickers (Making Memories); definition accent (My Mind's Eye); photo corner (Heidi Swapp); corner rounder

Daughter

Rachel Greig
Glenning Valley, New South Wales, Australia

Supplies: Cardstock; chipboard letters and words, patterned paper (Scenic Route); thread; pen

227

Great Scrapbook Idea!

Don't keep your scrapbooking to yourself! Use your talent to create a special gift for a friend or relative. While they may not be a scrapbooker, they will certainly appreciate the effort you put into making a custom-made gift, as Lisa has done with this layout she created for her friend. Your scrapbook gifts will become cherished keepsakes for years to come!

One Day

Lisa Tutman-Oglesby
Mundelein, Illinois

Supplies: Cardstock; patterned paper (Chatterbox, Creative Imaginations); chipboard letters, rub-on accents (Heidi Swapp); photo corners (BasicGrey); ribbon (American Crafts); flowers (Prima); acrylic paint; safety pin (Making Memories); buttons (Autumn Leaves); stamp (Stampendous); chulk ink; chalk; thread; transparency

Brouwer, Party of Six

Shannon Brouwer
Gilbert, Arizona

Supplies: Cardstock; patterned paper (My Mind's Eye); chipboard letters and arrow (Heidi Swapp); flower charm, tag (Li'l Davis); chipboard number (Rusty Pickle); chalk ink; button; die-cut accent (Sassafras Lass); rhinestones; pen

Reasons I Love My Daddy

Becky Teichmiller
Mukwonago, Wisconsin

Supplies: Cardstock; patterned paper (BasicGrey); die-cut letters (BasicGrey, QuicKutz); chipboard letters, rhinestone frame (Heidi Swapp); letter stickers (Making Memories); stamps (Autumn Leaves); plastic hearts (American Crafts); flowers, rhinestone border (Prima); chipboard circle (Urban Lily); buttons; pen

Mini-Me

Becky Teichmiller
Mukwonago, Wisconsin

Supplies: Cardstock; patterned paper, felt and letter accents (Tinkering Ink); scalloped cardstock (Bazzill); flowers (Prima); rub-on accents, stamps (Autumn Leaves); thread; pen

I Needed That

Maria Burke
Steinbach, Manitoba, Canada

Supplies: Cardstock; buttons, letter stickers, patterned paper (SEI); felt accents (Dollarama); corner rounder; SP You've Got Mail font (Internet download)

His Buddy

Nicole Stark
Roy, Utah

Supplies: Cardstock; patterned paper (Li'l Davis, Scenic Route); chipboard letters (Heidi Swapp); pigment ink; star rhinestones (unknown); pen

Great Scrapbook Idea!

Glancing through your stash, you'll likely find a bunch of old stickers and die cuts you can't see yourself ever using. Instead of tossing them, alter them! Doodling with pens, or adding glitter and paint is a great way to completely change the look of those worn out has-beens, turning them once again into the perfect page addition!

Daddy's Little Boy

Grace Castillo
Anaheim, California

Supplies: Cardstock; die-cut shapes, patterned paper, sticker accents (Pebbles); buttons, stamp (Autumn Leaves); rub-on accents and words (7gypsies, BasicGrey, Doodlebug); brads; twine; stamping ink; pen

Love

Kelly Bryan
Avon Lake, Ohio

Supplies: Cardstock; patterned paper (Scenic Route); flowers, metal letters, rub-on letters and stitches (American Crafts); brads; die-cut tag (My Mind's Eye); tag

Blissful Moment

Ivette Valladares
Aventura, Florida

Supplies: Cardstock; patterned paper (Chatterbox); chipboard letters (Making Memories); chipboard accent (Jenni Bowlin); buttons (Jo-Ann's); flowers (Making Memories, Prima); bookplate (BasicGrey); thread; Hurricane font (Internet download)

Great Scrapbook Idea!

You don't have to spend a lot of money to get those perfect chipboard accents! In fact, with a bit of elbow grease, you can make your own. Simply trace your design onto a piece of chipboard and cut it out with sharp scissors or a craft knife. You can create any design you please!

Finally Comprehending

Catherine Feegel-Erhardt
Tampa, Florida

Supplies: Cardstock; patterned paper (BasicGrey); stamping ink; chipboard; rhinestones; pen

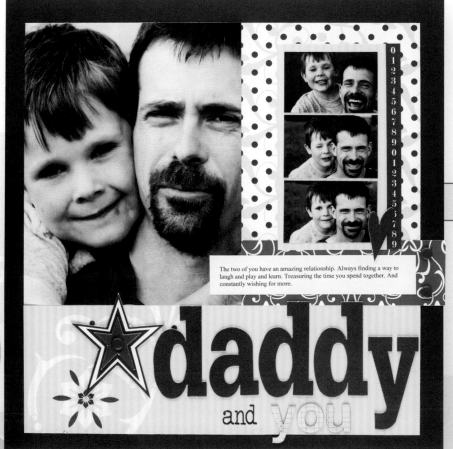

Daddy and You

Greta Hammond
Elkhart, Indiana

Supplies: Cardstock; chipboard shapes, patterned paper, rub-on letters (Imagination Project); chipboard letters (Heidi Swapp, Imagination Project); brads

Hands 2 Hold

Ivette Valladares
Aventura, Florida

*Supplies: Cardstock; patterned paper
(7gypsies, Fancy Pants, Jenni Bowlin);
corrugated paper (Paper Pizzaz); letter
stickers (Making Memories); rub-on accents
(BasicGrey); dye ink; corner rounder; pen*

Unconditional Love

Kay Rogers
Midland, Michigan

*Supplies: Die-cut shapes, patterned paper,
tags (My Mind's Eye); letter stickers (EK
Success); brads; ribbon (unknown)*

Great Scrapbook Idea!

You likely don't have the answers to all your children's questions, but it's okay, even therapeutic, to admit that on your layouts. Later in life, your children will thank you for your candor and your ability to admit you don't know everything. Don't be afraid to document your true feelings on your pages. No one wants to read about the life you dreamed you had. They want to know the real you!

Why?

Melita Ganoe
Jacksonville, Florida

Supplies: Patterned paper (BasicGrey); chipboard letters and accents (Fancy Pants); ribbon (unknown); ribbon slides (Maya Road); dye ink

Mommy & the Girls

Mary Anne Humes
Cheney, Washington

Supplies: Letter stickers, patterned paper (BasicGrey); stamps (Autumn Leaves); acrylic paint; corner rounder; thread; pen

This Is Us

Alissa Fast
Ferndale, Washington

Supplies: Patterned paper (Scenic Route); rub-on frame (Daisy D's); stamps (FontWerks, Li'l Davis); stamping ink; pen

Found

Katrina Simeck
Colchester, Vermont

Supplies: Cardstock; patterned paper (BasicGrey); chipboard letters (Chatterbox); chipboard accent, journaling card (Fancy Pants); ribbon (We R Memory Keepers); staple

Thanks Mom

Greta Hammond
Elkhart, Indiana

Supplies: Cardstock; patterned paper, rub-on letters (Creative Imaginations, Fancy Pants); chipboard letters and shapes (Fancy Pants); plastic letters (Heidi Swapp); buttons (Autumn Leaves); acrylic paint

Thank you for the wisdom you have instilled in me.

Thanks you for the unconditional love and support you have shown.

Thank you for the guidance and knowledge as I enter into my own trials as a mother.

Thank you for always being there whether or not you agree with my decisions.

Thank you for being part of our lives on a daily basis even though you are miles away.

Thank you Mom for everything you do and everything you are. I couldn't do it all without you.

I love you

THANKS Mom

Birdlegs

Sue Fields
South Whitley, Indiana

Supplies: Cardstock; chipboard letters, patterned paper, sticker accents (KI Memories); chipboard accents (KI Memories, Magistical Memories); stamp (Li'l Davis); stamping ink

Dad and I actually started out having a conversation about the Super bowl you know, the one where the COLTS became World Champs in 2007. We got off the subject and were talking about how cold it had been. It was a week where the high temps were below 10 degrees. Out of the blue, Dad mentioned how sorry he felt for the little birds standing in the snow, trying to get food from underneath the feeder. He said something about their tiny, little legs and feet must be FREEZING out there in the snow. He just couldn't imagine how they kept warm. It was if their legs might be like icicles and break right off. I had to chuckle, as only Dad would wonder why birds' legs don't break off in the cold. Good ol' Dad, he never stops questioning and learning, even at 80!

yawn purr tweet

chirp

tweet

tweet

I Love You Pops!

Suzy Plantamura
Laguna Niguel, California

Supplies: Cardstock; patterned paper (Me & My Big Ideas, My Mind's Eye, Sassafras Lass); chipboard letters, stitched stickers (unknown); rub-on stitches (We R Memory Keepers); transparency (Hambly); chalk ink; stamp (Hero Arts); pen

A Man to Look up To

Courtney Walsh
Winnebago, Illinois

Supplies: Patterned paper (Autumn Leaves); letter stickers (American Crafts); flowers (Prima); floss; pigment ink; pen

best of times

There's nothing more important than family And when these two get together they show just how much they truly love each other ♥ It makes me so happy I hope it lasts forever

never let go

sweet

Great Scrapbook Idea!

For a fun twist on the same old journaling, try this creative technique: Intersperse your own typed or handwritten words with decorative word stickers, rub-ons or chipboard accents. It not only breaks up the text, it dresses up any layout.

Sweet

Lisa Tutman-Oglesby
Mundelein, Illinois

Supplies: Cardstock; patterned paper (Heidi Grace); chipboard letters, rhinestones (Heidi Swapp); rub-on letters (Creative Imaginations); ribbon (Making Memories); word stickers (Heidi Grace, Making Memories); thread

ready

go!

Funny how it's only a race if Chase says it's a race—and Chase always wins! But this time, Kylie decided to trick him. They both started running and she gave Chase the slip by quickly turning around and running back to the starting line. I'm sure in her mind she won this time, but Chase insisted "it wasn't a race." The second time around, Chase made sure he stayed behind Kylie just in case she decided to try to "win" again.

Sculpture Park
April 29, 2006

Ready-Set-Go!

Becky Fleck
Columbus, Montana
Photos by: Tricia Ribble

Supplies: Cardstock; chipboard letters, patterned paper (KI Memories); ribbon (Shoebox Trims); acrylic paint; flower sequins (Doodlebug)

Tickle You

Lisa Carroll
Asheville, North Carolina

Supplies: Cardstock; die-cut shapes, patterned paper (Bam Pop); letter stickers (Heidi Swapp); decorative punches (Provo Craft); pen

Proud Brother

Maureen Spell
Muncie, Indiana

Supplies: Digital papers (Jen Wilson); butterfly (Sweet Shoppe); journal lines (Designer Digitals); Hand Note font (Jen Wilson); Typenoksidi font (Dafont)

Friends

Becky Thackston
Hiram, Georgia

Supplies: Cardstock; patterned paper (BasicGrey); letter stickers (American Crafts); stamps (Autumn Leaves); acrylic paint; brads; stamping ink; pen

Unconditional

Maria Burke
Steinbach, Manitoba, Canada

Supplies: Cardstock; patterned paper (BasicGrey, SEI); letter stickers, tab (SEI); butterfly (Dollarama); corner rounder; pen; 2Peas Journaling Dingbats (Two Peas in a Bucket); My Own Topher font (Internet download)

Together

Becky Novacek
Fremont, Nebraska

Supplies: Cardstock; patterned paper (Anna Griffin, Scenic Route); letter stickers (Li'l Davis); ribbon (Offray); stamp (FontWerks); stamping ink; decorative scissors; staples; pen

Sweet Kisses

Virginia Powell
Jackson, Georgia

Supplies: Cardstock; patterned paper (My Mind's Eye); rub-on letters and words (Colorbok, Doodlebug); metal flowers (unknown); paper flowers (Fancy Pants); plastic flowers (Heidi Grace); rickrack; brads; stamping ink; pen

Great Scrapbook Idea!

If you love using flowers, but want something more than the usual, try adding stitches to your layout. Hand stitching stems is an easy way to add texture and dimension and gives your flowers a little something extra. You can also stitch around the centers or outsides of the flowers for added detail.

I Heart My Sister

Gretchen McElveen
Helena, Alabama

Supplies: Cardstock; patterned paper (Scenic Route); letter stickers (Doodlebug); chipboard hearts (American Crafts); floss; pen

S🯅🯅sters Camille and Danielle, You two are as different as you are the same! You are both sweet and caring, imaginitive...you love to giggle, to eat pepperoni pizza, play soccer, do crafts, and paint your nails. Danielle, you are a type B personality as much as your sister is a type A. Camille you are most happy with a neat and clean space; whereas Danielle, you are satisfied with "organized chaos." Camille loves to be on stage, where Danielle you prefer a smaller setting to perform in. Your differences compliment one another...I'm glad you get along so well!

Great Scrapbook Idea!

So many symbols have become an integral part of our culture, we don't always see them as possible additions to our designs. Adding these well-known signs is a great way to incorporate your everyday world into a layout. Look for ways to include recognizable symbols in your designs for a fun, modern look!

Sisters

Samantha Walker
Lehi, Utah

Supplies: Digital elements and overlay (artist's own design); image editing software (Adobe); Helvetica font (Microsoft)

Swing

Michelle Cathcart
Sugar Grove, Pennsylvania

Supplies: Cardstock; patterned paper (KI Memories, Scenic Route); numbers (Sassafras Lass paper); chipboard letters, transparent stars (Heidi Swapp); rhinestones (Westrim); pigment ink; pen

Pals

Grace Castillo
Anaheim, California

*Supplies: Cardstock; patterned paper
(Imagination Project); pen*

Friends

**Cari Fennell
DeWitt, New York**

*Supplies: Scalloped cardstock
(Bazzill); patterned paper (KI
Memories, SEI); chipboard
letters (Scenic Route); decorative
punches (Marvy, McGill); buttons
(Autumn Leaves); ribbon (Offray);
acrylic paint; thread; pen*

Great Scrapbook Idea!

You may have a particular scrapbooking style, but sometimes it doesn't suit your photos. Consider allowing your photos to choose the style for a page, like choosing a vintage look for old photos. Design a layout that complements your photos even if it's outside your comfort zone. You may surprise yourself with the results!

Sisters

Lisa Tutman-Oglesby
Mundelein, Illinois

Supplies: Cardstock; patterned paper (Anna Griffin, NRN Designs); chipboard letters (Heidi Swapp, Making Memories); chipboard and rub-on accents (Fancy Pants); acrylic paint; transparency; thread

Might As Well Be Sisters

Katrina Simeck
Colchester, Vermont

Supplies: Cardstock; die-cut letters, patterned paper (BasicGrey); flowers (Prima); adhesive foam; brads; pen

Not So Fast Friends

Courtney Walsh
Winnebago, Illinois

Supplies: Digital buttons, flower, paper and stitches (Shabby Princess); inked edge (Designer Digitals); Prissy Frat Boy, Susie's Hand, Trebuchet fonts (Internet download)

Carrie and I weren't always great friends. She is, after all, my little sister. When we were growing up, we fought ALL THE TIME. She says I was 'so mean' and I say she was 'so annoying.' I'm not quite sure when things changed. Maybe when I stopped seeing her as a little kid. Now, Carrie is one of my best friends.

She is someone I could trust with my life. Someone who I know will never betray me or let me down. I am so thankful I've got a baby sister... even though these days, she's anything but a baby.

Our relationship is one of understanding. And even though she's younger than me, she's the person (aside from Adam) who I most turn to for advice. I hope over the years, this friendship will just continue to grow. Somehow, I think there's no stopping it.

Not so Fast Friends

the oldest, the youngest, lives so different while growing up, and lives so different now. but being adults and being parents have given marc and laura common ground, and they are now closer than ever.

Being (Grown-Ups) Together

Michele Skinner
Burnsville, Minnesota

Supplies: Cardstock; patterned paper (Crafter's Workshop); letter stickers (Chatterbox); rub-on letters and words (Daisy D's, Making Memories); negative frames (Creative Imaginations); tag (7gypsies); staples; pen

Three

Brooke Bartimioli
Hayden, Idaho

Supplies: Patterned paper (Daisy D's, Karen Foster, Urban Lily, Wube); stamps (Inkadinkado); stamping ink; letter stickers (EK Success, Making Memories); rub-on letters (Daisy D's); small tag (Staples); large tag (clothing tag); brads; rope; twine; pen

The nice thing about having a sister is you always have a best friend around. In the best and worst times we have always been there for each other and we will always be best friends forever.

B.F.F.

Crystal Jeffrey Rieger
Woodbridge, Ontario, Canada

Supplies: Digital letter brushes, frame (ScrapArtist); floral and flourish brushes, patterned paper (Oscraps); Century Gothic font (Microsoft)

Anecdote

April Foster
Bowling Green, Kentucky

Supplies: Cardstock; patterned paper (KI Memories); letter stickers (Li'l Davis); brads; rub-on accents (7gypsies, BasicGrey); star (Heidi Swapp); tab (EK Success); pen

1942
anecDOTe WWII

Love Always

Kim Moreno
Tucson, Arizona

Supplies: Cardstock; patterned paper (Three Bugs in a Rug); chipboard word (Li'l Davis); twill (Scenic Route); brads; pigment ink; decorative scissors

G'pa and Kenna

Just to look at these sweet pictures melts my heart. I took them during our visit to Texas on our way to our new house in Arizona. You had not seen your Gpa in about 2 years when these pictures were taken, we had been stationed in Germany. What a sweet moment this was to see the two of you bond like this like there had been no time between you two. I would love to know the sweet secrets that you two seem to be whispering to each other. I hope you remember these moments Makenna, because they are so special! You see as I journal this I am in tears thinking of what will never be, your Gpa passed away just a week ago today. I worry that you will never remember the love he had for you and how special you were to him. You were his sweet "Kenny-Mac" and he was one of your biggest fans. The relationship the two of you had might have been short but it was so very special and unique. When I look at these pictures one word comes to mind: LOVE. He loved you so much Kenna and he always will. Photos taken July 2005 and journaled on July 12, 2006.

Great Scrapbook Idea!

No more wallflowers on your pages! Make a statement with your handmade embellishments by making them larger than life. Look for ways to turn other page essentials like your title, journaling or a series of small photos into super-sized design elements for a bold, dynamic look!

Picking Flowers with Grandma

Suzy Plantamura
Laguna Niguel, California

Supplies: Cardstock; patterned paper (Autumn Leaves, WorldWin); letter stickers (BasicGrey); fibers (unknown); pen

Ammy is Our Granny

Shannon Taylor
Bristol, Tennessee

Supplies: Cardstock; patterned paper (My Mind's Eye); letter stickers (American Crafts); chipboard frame (Fancy Pants); patterned transparency (Hambly); staples

Date with Papa

Maria Durke
Steinbach, Manitoba, Canada

Supplies: Cardstock; patterned paper (Making Memories, SEI); epoxy sticker, letter stickers, ribbon, tag, velvet paper (SEI); rub-on stitches (Die Cuts With A View); pen; 2Peas Falling Leaves font (Two Peas in a Bucket)

you had so much fun on your date with papa. He took you into the city just the two of you to see Ice Age 2. He bought you your very own popcorn and drink. He even surprised you with a stuffed Manny. I love that you two have such a special relationship and go on special "dates" just the two of you. Sarah, you have no idea how much your papa loves you!!

li'l mikey gets a big kiss from mimi

Kiss

Staci Compher
Carleton, Michigan

Supplies: Cardstock; patterned paper (Autumn Leaves, Daisy D's); chipboard letters (Chatterbox); rhinestone heart (Me & My Big Ideas); ribbon (Jo-Ann's, May Arts); buttons; staples; pen

grandmother

Grandmother

Deborah Liu
Santa Clara, California

Supplies: Cardstock; fibers, key accents (Maya Road); pen

A Big Part of Your Life

Greta Hammond
Elkhart, Indiana

Supplies: Cardstock; chipboard accents, patterned paper, rickrack (Fancy Pants); chipboard letters (Fancy Pants, Heidi Swapp); rub-on letters (Making Memories); acrylic paint; brads; rhinestones (My Mind's Eye)

Great Scrapbook Idea!

One way to create a well-designed layout is to include a visual triangle, which creates a boundary for the eye, linking all the elements together. The use of a color, like Melanie's choice of green, can act as a visual triangle as can the use of embellishments. This simple design tip will give your layouts a unified look every time!

Together

Melanie McFarlin
Lewisville, Texas

Supplies: Cardstock; patterned paper (Scenic Route); chipboard flowers (Everlasting Keepsakes); chipboard swirls (Maya Road); buttons (SEI); rickrack; stamping ink

I just *love* this picture of you and your nana, smiling so sweetly.

We don't get to see your grandparents as much as we would like,

but I know they love you and miss you very much.

Christmas, 2005

Retrouvailles

Champagne Severine
Dolomieu, France

Supplies: Digital cardstock (ScrapArtist); patterned paper (Shabby Princess); brush (Creepy Dolly); image editing software (Adobe); Carpenter ICG, Deco P700, Roselyn fonts (Internet download)

Susan Weinroth
Centerville, Minnesota

Supplies: Cardstock; buttons, patterned paper (American Crafts); chipboard heart, die-cut letters, rub-on accents (Heidi Grace); brads; decorative punch; corner rounder; floss

Great Scrapbook Idea!

Even the tiniest embellishments make a big statement when showcased in bulk! Susan's heart border is comprised of several small punched hearts with mini-brads at the centers. These tiny elements might have been lost standing on their own, but lined up, they create a dynamic addition to the page.

Adoration

Pam Callaghan
Bowling Green, Ohio

Supplies: Cardstock; patterned paper (Tinkering Ink); flowers (Prima); brads; thread

Sean and his grandmother simple adore one another. Sean is Grandma Hasting's first grandchild. She loves to spend time reading, playing cards, and tickling him. Grandma simply loves to be around Sean and has a tendency to spoil him. She is always bringing him toys, buying clothes for him, and slipping him way to much chocolate. But that is to be expected.

Adoration

Sean is always incredibly happy when Grandma Hastings comes to visit. He greets her at door with a big hug and kiss. Sean is always excited during grandma's stay, perhaps because she often spoils him. For the next few days, he will ask where is Grandma as soon as he gets up the morning. He loves to play with her and is constantly hugging her throughout the day. When she leaves Sean is sad for the rest of the day. But that is to be expected.

I love the relationship that my mom has with all my children. They adore spending time with her and somehow she always manages to find the time to give each child individual attention. This picture of Isaac sitting quietly with her on the bank of a lake at the campground is one of the few moments I have ever captured of him sitting still. Bom's soft voice and gentle manner helped him stop for a minute and listen intently to what she was saying. I am so glad that I was able to capture this quiet moment of them. We are so lucky that she is such an important part of their lives.

06

Bom and Isaac

Quiet
MOMENTS

Quiet Moments

Kathy Fesmire
Athens, Tennessee

Supplies: Cardstock; patterned paper (My Mind's Eye); rub-on accents (Dee's Designs); metal accents (Queen & Co.); wooden accents (Li'l Davis); ribbons (EK Success, Offray); chalk ink

Ahhh... the joys of being a girl. The boys were gone to play golf, leaving just us girls at the house to hang out. Grandma decided that it would be a great time to indulge you with one of your favorite things— a spa day- complete with a manicure and a pedicure. You chose a rose color for your toes and a soft pink for your fingers. You are such a girly girl and love being pampered by grandma!

July 2006

a spa day with
grandma

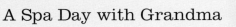

A Spa Day with Grandma

Tracie Radtke
Chicago, Illinois

Supplies: Digital kit (ScrapArtist); note paper (Twisted Lollipop); image editing software (Adobe); LD Fierro, LD Thankful, Pea Shirley fonts (Internet download)

Strive to Make a Difference

Lisa Tilmon
Rogers, Arkansas

Supplies: Cardstock; chipboard letters and accent, patterned paper (Scenic Route); buttons (MOD); pin (Heidi Grace); number sticker (American Crafts); ribbon, tag (Stampin' Up); Tahoma font (Microsoft)

Family Is

April Foster
Bowling Green, Kentucky

Supplies: Cardstock; letter stickers, rub-on accents, stamps (KI Memories); stamping ink; photo corners; pen

Family Time

Samantha Walker
Lehi, Utah

Supplies: Kraft cardstock; cardstock; patterned paper (Around the Block); letter stickers (Chatterbox); chipboard accents, digital border (Karen Russell); hole punch; pen

It is so great to watch you four together. Even though you live in different cities whenever you are together it is like you never parted. There are giggles & laughter & the occasional fight but all in all you have fun

Wonderland

Ride Smart... Ride Safe

152cm/60" AND UP

137cm/54" AND UP

122cm/48" AND UP

cousins

June, 2006

Magnus (2), Artemis (6), Jonah (4), Harper (9)

Cousins

Crystal Jeffrey Rieger
Woodbridge, Ontario, Canada

Supplies: Cardstock; ribbons (Michaels); stamps (Gelatins); pigment ink; brads, eyelets, snaps (Making Memories); chipboard heart (BasicGrey); decorative scissors (Provo Craft); pen

Kitten Kisses

Sandra Stanton
Northfield, New Jersey

Supplies: Digital page kit, brushes, date stamp, letter beads (Digi Chick); beaded elements (LilyPad); shadow actions (Traci Murphy); Diesel, Downcome, Pea Jenny Script fonts (Internet download)

kitten
KISSES

You and Babe have become best buds! I catch the two of you having quiet time together on Mommy & Daddy's bed. Babe gives you kisses!

JAN 07

MEOW

Loyal Buddy

Jill Cornell
Windsor Heights, Iowa

Supplies: Cardstock; patterned paper, tag accents (Karen Foster); letter stickers (American Crafts); ribbon; button (Autumn Leaves); paw print accents (artist's own design); pen

BoCo was Glen's best buddy for 14 years. BoCo helped him through some very tough times and was a very sweet friend.

I'M ADORABLE

DOGS LEAVE PAWPRINTS ON YOUR

loyal BUDDY

What we have here is a pint-sized pug with a penchant for face lotion and a rapid-fire smoochie reflex and a girl who tries desperately not to think about germs. (2006)

puppy smoochie

Puppy Smoochie

Mary MacAskill
Calgary, Alberta, Canada

Supplies: Cardstock; patterned paper (Imagination Project); ribbon, rub-on accent (American Crafts); brad; corner rounder; thread

A Fish Named Sally

Alison Lockett
Knoxville, Tennessee

Supplies: Cardstock; patterned paper (Creative Imaginations, Scenic Route); chipboard letters (Fancy Pants); stamps (Sassafras Lass); photo corners (Daisy D's); decorative tape (Heidi Swapp); chipboard stars (Li'l Davis); flower (Prima); pen

Burton

Catherine Feegel-Erhardt
Tampa, Florida

Supplies: Cardstock; patterned paper (Paper House, Scenic Route); ribbon (American Crafts, Offray); brads; glitter; stamping ink; acrylic paint; rub-on accents (Li'l Davis); adhesive foam; stamp (Technique Tuesday); staples; pen

Shine Rascy Shine

Kristen Jo Rousch
Madison, Indiana

Supplies: Cardstock; patterned paper (American Crafts, KI Memories, Scenic Route); letter stickers (American Crafts, KI Memories, Making Memories); stamps (Autumn Leaves); solvent ink; chalk ink; photo corners; rickrack (Wrights); pen

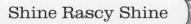

Lucky Dawg

Janine Wahl
Sylvan Lake, Alberta, Canada

Supplies: Cardstock; patterned paper (BasicGrey, Karen Foster); acrylic paint; chipboard letters (Heidi Swapp, Pressed Petals); chipboard accents (Fancy Pants); sequin flowers (Queen & Co.); brads; buttons; transparency; pen

Buster is quite the character. He is content. He is charming. He is calm, to the point that he is almost passive. He is happy-go-lucky. Especially the ____ part.

He has been grazed by a poacher's bullet. He has almost been run-over. He's been sprayed by skunks countless times. He's recovered from hind leg paralysis, twice!

After thirteen years, he is still alive and kickin', living life with a puppy's heart.

LUCKY DAWG
MAY 2006

Mogs

Trudy Sigurdson
Victoria, British Columbia, Canada

Supplies: Cardstock; chipboard accents, patterned paper, rub-on letters (Imagination Project); acrylic letters (Memories Complete); rub-on shapes (Polar Bear Press); acrylic circles (Heidi Grace); die-cut numbers (QuicKutz); photo anchors (7gypsies); stamping ink; dimensional glaze; brads; adhesive foam; thread; Fastpardon font (Internet download); Verdana font (Microsoft)

christmas day 2005

mogs

Gentle eyes that see so much,
Paws that have the quiet touch,
Purrs to signal "all is well"
And show more love than words could tell.
Graceful movements touched with pride,
A calming presence by our side,
A friendship that takes time to grow
Small wonder why we love Mogs so.

Great Scrapbook Idea!

You've likely got scraps upon scraps piling up in your stash. Don't get rid of them until you consider this fun technique. Using just small squares or circles of various coordinating patterned paper, you can create a great impact on your layout as Sandi proves. This is the perfect border as it doesn't distract from the photos or overwhelm the page.

Full of Life

Sandi Minchuk
Merrillville, Indiana

Supplies: Scalloped cardstock (Bazzill); patterned paper (Paper Loft); letter stickers (Making Memories); dye ink; transparency (Transparent Touches); thread

Great Scrapbook Idea!

Give your silk and paper flowers double the volume with a simple fold. By folding flowers in half and tucking them behind other design elements, you'll add texture and depth giving the floral embellishments a presence on the page. And by cutting the size in half, you'll keep flowers from overwhelming the layout.

Taylor

Kerry Zerff
Regina, Saskatchewan, Canada

Supplies: Cardstock; chipboard bookplate, patterned paper (BasicGrey); flower (Prima); brads (Making Memories); stamps (Gelatins); embossing powder; stamping ink; thread; pen

The Magic of Having a Neighbor

Diane D. Michael
Mannington, West Virginia

Supplies: Digital page kit (ScrapArtist)

JOY

Years ago we made the decision not to go the Suburbia USA route. We were concerned that our children would only be exposed to people of similar socio-economic status and belief systems. So we now live in the country. You know what that means- no close neighbors with kids your age, no built in playmates. Play dates are set up in advance, carefully planned. Your nearest friend is a fifteen minute drive. Visiting Uncle Seth and the kids opened up a whole new world for you. Surburbia USA. Yes, even with its requisite designer homes, carefully manicured lawns, and driveways full of SUVs, we discovered that suburban life had one wonderful quality that we had overlooked- wide open play invitations. My brother and his family live in a neighborhood full of wonderful families, led by parents who truly want their children to have a magical childhood. Michael, the kids in your cousin Eric's neighborhood have a great thing going, and for the week that we visited, you reveled in the open door policy - boys going back and forth between each other's houses, a rec room with a bar set up for the kids - stocked with snacks and drinks, and babysitters and stay-at-home parents who made cupcakes and took you on wonderful adventures. Then, of course, there was the exposure to early morning swim team practices, Yu-Gi-Oh and Pokemon duels, backyard water fights, and built in tree houses. You absolutely gloried in the comradeship, the simple pleasures of an enchanted childhood- all found within a two block perimeter. Summer 2004.

ADVENTURE worthwhile.

BLOOM BLOOM BLOOM

hanging with friends

the magic of having a NEIGHBOR

GiRlfriends

Kendall and Delaney just love being together. Here they are just hanging out, playing, and being silly for the camera. I love the personality shown in these shots! Fort Wilderness Campground, November 2006

Girlfriends

Annemarie Mackin
Safety Harbor, Florida

Supplies: Cardstock; patterned paper (Scenic Route); letter stickers (KI Memories); flower brads, large flowers (Making Memories); brads; circle punch

1st Friendship

Catherine Feegel-Erhardt
Tampa, Florida

Supplies: Cardstock; patterned paper (Die Cuts With A View); ribbon (American Crafts, Offray); stamping ink; adhesive foam; pen

An Unusual Sort of Friendship

Hillary Heidelberg
New York, New York

Supplies: Cardstock; rub-on letters (Doodlebug); brads; Freaking Stars, Traditianelle Sans fonts (Internet downloads); Impact font (Microsoft)

2000 miles
scrappin'
toilet training
partner in crime
girlie time
text messages
late nights
lol
support
teaching together
friend*
daily emails

Great Scrapbook Idea!

Sometimes just a spot of color makes a greater impact on a page than several bold, colorful elements. To allow a certain word or photo to take center stage, consider coloring just the one element and keeping the rest of the layout neutral. This is an effective way to ensure that element remains the focus.

Friend

Crystal Jeffrey Rieger
Woodbridge, Ontario, Canada

Supplies: Image editing software (Adobe); Impact font (Microsoft)

At a time when I really needed to laugh, I got to go out for a night on the town with my friends. I haven't had this much fun in a LONG time! These girls truly know how to laugh... and that's one of the most important things in any relationship! We went to PF Chang's in downtown Chicago. The food was AMAZING. Then dessert was even better... but it was the company that would have me coming back for seconds! I'm so lucky to have these girls in my life. I can't wait to do it again soon! March * 2007*

Girlfriends

Courtney Walsh
Winnebago, Illinois

Supplies: Digital flowers, paper (Jessica Sprague); inked edge (Two Peas in a Bucket); Susie's Hand, Trebuchet fonts (Internet download)

Greta Hammond
Elkhart, Indiana

Supplies: Cardstock; chipboard letters, patterned paper; rub-on letters (Scenic Route); letter stickers (Making Memories); buttons (Autumn Leaves); rhinestones (Heidi Swapp); digital frame (Two Peas in a Bucket); adhesive foam

unexpected friend

I never thought a hobby like scrapbooking would bring such an amazing friend into my life. The moment I met Vicki, I knew that we would be friends. Even though we live miles apart, thanks to technology we "chat" almost daily and meet at trade shows every few months. We are so much in common and are so much alike, sometimes it is scary! I am so grateful for the friendship and support she has given me in the past year. It would have been a lonely road without her on the other side of my computer screen. Love ya Vicki!

Friend

Courtney Kelly
Anchorage, Alaska

Supplies: Cardstock; chipboard letters, patterned paper (Scenic Route); photo turns (American Crafts); brads; Highlight font (Autumn Leaves)

friend

LOTS OF LATE NIGHT PHONE CALLS, GIGGLING NON-STOP, WAY TOO MANY "DUDES" IN THE CONVERSATION, BUT DUDE, I TOTALLY LOVE YOU LIKE A SISTER.

Great Scrapbook Idea!

Recreate the look of yesteryear on your layout in a snap. First, print your photo (or have it printed) with a white border. Then cut around the edge of the border with deckle-edge scissors. Adding black photo corners will enhance the old-time look.

Playmates

Linda Beeson
Ventura, California

Supplies: Cardstock; patterned paper (WorldWin); letter stickers (Creative Imaginations); photo corners; chalk ink; large brads (Bazzill); decorative punch; thread

Like Sisters

Melanie Douthit
West Monroe, Louisiana

Supplies: Cardstock; brads, buttons, patterned paper, ribbon (Hot Off The Press); rub-on words (Scenic Route); stamping ink; thread

Hello Beep Beep

Alissa Fast
Ferndale, Washington

Supplies: Patterned paper (Scenic Route); stamps (FontWerks); die-cut letters (QuicKutz); rhinestones; pen

"HELLO BEEP BEEP

I guess I should explain: my mom has taken to calling birds "Beep Beep". It all started with her feeding the birds that come into her yard. I think she said one of the varieties of woodpeckers make that sound "Beep Beep", So, she calls them "Beep Beep" and just about any other bird we see. Silly, I know! That's why I've started calling her "The Crazy Bird Lady" and she loves it! Lol!

Memory Makers Masters

Catherine Feegel-Erhardt
Tampa, Florida

Supplies: Cardstock; patterned paper (Tinkering Ink); letter stickers (US Stamp & Sign); brad; button; flower (cut from chipboard); adhesive foam; pen

We entered! We won great prizes! The best prize was friendship!

A Community of friendship & Creativity

Memory makers MASTERS

SCRAPBOOKING

JANUARY 2007

12 Months

Creative On Demand

5 instant FRIENDS

ULTIMATE!

Design TEAM MEET and PLAY at CHA

CRYSTAL · MICHELE · CATHERINE · KATRINA · RONEE

Source Guide

The following companies manufacture products featured in this book. Please check your local retailers to find these materials, or go to a company's Web site for the latest product information. In addition, we have made every attempt to properly credit the items mentioned in this book. We apologize to any company that we have listed incorrectly, and we would appreciate hearing from you.

3L Corporation
(800) 828-3130
www.scrapbook-adhesives.com

3M
(800) 364-3577
www.3m.com

7gypsies
(877) 749-7797
www.sevengypsies.com

A2Z Essentials
(419) 663-2869
www.geta2z.com

Adobe Systems Incorporated
(800) 833-6687
www.adobe.com

Adorn It / Carolee's Creations
(435) 563-1100
www.adornit.com

Agnes Lahur Designs
www.agnes.lahur.com/shoppe

All My Memories
(888) 553-1998
www.allmymemories.com

American Crafts
(801) 226-0747
www.americancrafts.com

American Tag Company
(800) 223-3956
www.americantag.net

American Traditional Designs
(800) 448-6656
www.americantraditional.com

Anna Griffin, Inc.
(888) 817-8170
www.annagriffin.com

ANW Crestwood
(973) 406-5000
www.anwcrestwood.com

Arctic Frog
(479) 636-3764
www.arcticfrog.com

Around The Block
(801) 593-1946
www.aroundtheblockproducts.com

Atomic Cupcake
www.atomiccupcake.com

Autumn Leaves
(800) 588-6707
www.autumnleaves.com

Avery Dennison Corporation
(800) 462-8379
www.avery.com

BAM POP LLC
www.bampop.com

BasicGrey
(801) 544-1116
www.basicgrey.com

Bazzill Basics Paper
(480) 558-8557
www.bazzillbasics.com

Beaux Regards
(203) 438-1105
www.beauxregards.com

Berwick Offray, LLC
(800) 344-5533
www.offray.com

BIC World
www.bicworld.com

Bisous
www.bisousscrapbooks.com

Bobarbo
(418) 748-6775
www.bobarbo.com

Bo-Bunny Press
(801) 771-4010
www.bobunny.com

Boxer Scrapbook Productions, LLC
(888) 625-6255
www.boxerscrapbooks.com

Brother International Corporation
www.brother-usa.com

Buttons Galore & More
(856) 753-6700
www.buttonsgaloreandmore.com

Buzz and Bloom
www.buzzandbloom.com.au

CatScrap
www.catscrap.com

Catslife Press
(541) 902-7855
www.harborside.com/~catslife/

Cavallini Papers & Co., Inc.
(800) 226-5287
www.cavallini.com

ChartPak
(800) 628-1910
www.chartpak.com

Chatterbox, Inc.
(888) 416-6260
www.chatterboxinc.com

CherryArte
(212) 465-3495
www.cherryarte.com

Close To My Heart
(888) 655-6552
www.closetomyheart.com

Cloud 9 Design
(866) 348-5661
www.cloud9design.biz

Club Scrap, Inc.
(888) 634-9100
www.clubscrap.com

Coats & Clark
(800) 648-1479
www.coatsandclark.com

Colorbök, Inc.
(800) 366-4660
www.colorbok.com

Cosmo Cricket
(800) 852-8810
www.cosmocricket.com

Crafter's Workshop, The
(877) 272-3837
www.thecraftersworkshop.com

Crate Paper
(801) 798-8996
www.cratepaper.com

Creative Imaginations
(800) 942-6487
www.cigift.com

Creative Impressions, Inc.
(719) 596-4860
www.creativeimpressions.com

Creative Memories
(800) 468-9335
www.creativememories.com

C-Thru Ruler Company, The
(800) 243-8419
www.cthruruler.com

Dafont
www.dafont.com

Daisy D's Paper Company
(888) 601-8955
www.daisydspaper.com

Darice, Inc.
(800) 321-1494
www.darice.com

DECAdry PC Papers
www.decadry.com

Dee's Designs
http://vij10.tripod.com/deesdesigns

Dèjá Views
(800) 243-8419
www.dejaviews.com

Deluxe Designs
(480) 497-9005
www.deluxecuts.com

Design Originals
(800) 877-0067
www.d-originals.com

Designer Digitals
www.designerdigitals.com

Die Cuts With A View
(801) 224-6766
www.diecutswithaview.com

Digi Chick, The
www.thedigichick.com

Digi Shoppe, The
www.thedigishoppe.com

DigiShopTalk.com
www.digishoptalk.com

Digital Design Essentials
www.digitaldesignessentials.com

Digital Paper Tearing
www.digitalpapertearing.com

Dollarstore, Inc.
(949) 261-7488
www.dollarstore.com

Dollarama - *no source available*

Doodlebug Design Inc.
(877) 800-9190
www.doodlebug.ws

Dream Street Papers
(480) 275-9736
www.dreamstreetpapers.com

Duncan Enterprises
(800) 438-6226
www.duncancrafts.com

Dutch Boy Group
www.dutchboy.com

Dymo
(800) 426-7827
www.dymo.com

EK Success, Ltd.
(800) 524-1349
www.eksuccess.com

Ellison
(800) 253-2238
www.ellison.com

Erikia Ghumm
www.erikiaghumm.com

Everlasting Keepsakes
(816) 896-7037
www.everlastinkeepsakes.com

Fancy Pants Designs, LLC
(801) 779-3212
www.fancypantsdesigns.com

Fiber Scraps
(215) 230-4905
www.fiberscraps.com

FishScraps.com
www.fishscraps.com

Fiskars, Inc.
(866) 348-5661
www.fiskars.com

Flair Designs
(888) 546-9990
www.flairdesignsinc.com

FontWerks
(604) 942-3105
www.fontwerks.com

Frances Meyer, Inc.
(413) 584-5446
www.francesmeyer.com

Funky Playground Designs
www.funkyplaygrounddesigns.com

gel•a•tins
(800) 393-2151
www.gelatinstamps.com

Grafix
(800) 447-2349
www.grafixarts.com

Greener Pastures
www.greenerpastures.co.nz

Hambly Studios
(800) 451-3999
www.hamblystudios.com

Happy Hammer, The
(720) 870-5248
www.thehappyhammer.com

Heidi Grace Designs, Inc.
(866) 348-5661
www.heidigrace.com

Heidi Swapp/Advantus Corporation
(904) 482-0092
www.heidiswapp.com

Hero Arts Rubber Stamps, Inc.
(800) 822-4376
www.heroarts.com

Hirschberg Schutz & Co., Inc.
(800) 221-8640

Hobby Lobby Stores, Inc.
www.hobbylobby.com

Holly VanDyne Designs
www.hollyvandynedesigns.com

Hot Off The Press, Inc.
(800) 227-9595
www.b2b.hotp.com

Imagination Project, Inc.
(888) 477-6532
www.imaginationproject.com

Imaginisce
(801) 908-8111
www.imaginisce.com

Impress Rubber Stamps
(206) 901-9101
www.impressrubberstamps.com

Inkadinkado Rubber Stamps
(800) 523-8452
www.inkadinkado.com

Jen Wilson Designs
www.jenwilsondesigns.com

Jenni Bowlin
www.jennibowlin.com

Jessica Sprague
http://spraguelab.squarespace.com

Jo-Ann Stores
www.joann.com

JudiKins
(310) 515-1115
www.judikins.com

Junkitz
(732) 792-1108
www.junkitz.com

Just Lia
www.justlia.com.br

K&Company
(888) 244-2083
www.kandcompany.com

Karen Foster Design
(801) 451-9779
www.karenfosterdesign.com

Karen Russell
www.karenrussell.typepad.com

Keeping Memories Alive/Scrapbooks.com
(800) 727-2726
www.scrapbooks.com

KI Memories
(972) 243-5595
www.kimemories.com

Knock Knock/Who's There, Inc.
(800) 656-5662
www.knockknock.biz

Krylon
(800) 457-9566
www.krylon.com

Lä Dé Dä
(225) 755-8899
www.ladeda.com

Leaving Prints
www.leavingprints.com

Li'l Davis Designs
(480) 223-0080
www.lildavisdesigns.com

LilyPad, The
www.the-lilypad.com

Little Black Dress Designs
(360) 897-8844
www.littleblackdressdesigns.com

Little Dreamer Designs
www.littledreamerdesigns.com

Loersch Corporation USA
(610) 264-5641
www.loersch.com

Luxe Designs
(972) 573-2120
www.luxedesigns.com

Magenta Rubber Stamps
(450) 922-5253
www.magentastyle.com

Magic Mesh
(651) 345-6374
www.magicmesh.com

Magic Scraps
(904) 482-0092
www.magicscraps.com

Magistical Memories
(818) 842-1540
www.magisticalmemories.com

Magnetic Poetry
(800) 370-7697
www.magneticpoetry.com

MaisyMo Designs
(973) 907-7262
www.maisymo.com

Making Memories
(801) 294-0430
www.makingmemories.com

Marvy Uchida/ Uchida of America, Corp.
(800) 541-5877
www.uchida.com

May Arts
(800) 442-3950
www.mayarts.com

Maya Road, LLC
(214) 488-3279
www.mayaroad.com

McGill, Inc.
(800) 982-9884
www.mcgillinc.com

me & my BiG ideas
(949) 583-2065
www.meandmybigideas.com

Melissa Frances/Heart & Home, Inc.
(888) 616-6166
www.melissafrances.com

Memories Complete, LLC
(866) 966-6365
www.memoriescomplete.com

Mermaid Tears
(310) 569-3345
www.mermaidtears.net

Michaels Arts & Crafts
(800) 642-4235
www.michaels.com

Microsoft Corporation
www.microsoft.com

Miss Elizabeth's - *no source available*

Misty Cato Designs
www.mistycatodesigns.blogspot.com

MOD — My Own Design
(303) 641-8680
www.mod-myowndesign.com

Morex Corporation
(717) 852-7771
www.morexcorp.com

Mrs. Grossman's Paper Company
(800) 429-4549
www.mrsgrossmans.com

Mustard Moon
(763) 493-5157
www.mustardmoon.com

My Digital Muse
www.mydigitalmuse.com

My Mind's Eye, Inc.
(800) 665-5116
www.mymindseye.com

NRN Designs
(800) 421-6958
www.nrndesigns.com

October Afternoon
www.octoberafternoon.com

Office Depot
www.officedepot.com

Offray - see Berwick Offray, LLC

Old Navy/Gap Inc. Brands
www.oldnavy.com

One Heart...One Mind, LLC
(888) 414-3690

Oscraps
www.oscraps.com

Paper Adventures - see ANW Crestwood

Paper Company, The - see ANW Crestwood

Paper House Productions
(800) 255-7316
www.paperhouseproductions.com

Paper Loft, The
(801) 254-1961
www.paperloft.com

Paper Mate/Sanford
(800) 323-0749
www.papermate.com

Paper Salon
(800) 627-2648
www.papersalon.com

Paper Studio
(480) 557-5700
www.paperstudio.com

Paper Tapestry
(608) 848-2172
www.papertapestry.com

Paperwerks
(866) 479-0868
www.paperwerks.com

Paperwhite
(888) 236-7400
www.paperwhitememories.com

Pebbles Inc.
(801) 235-1520
www.pebblesinc.com

Penny Black, Inc.
www.pennyblackinc.com

Pickleberrypop
www.pickleberrypop.com

Piggy Tales
(702) 755-8600
www.piggytales.com

Pink Martini Designs, LLC
(845) 228-5833
www.pinkmartinidesigns.com

Plaid Enterprises, Inc.
(800) 842-4197
www.plaidonline.com

Polar Bear Press
(801) 451-7670
www.polarbearpress.com

Poppy, Inc.
www.poppyinc.com

Pressed Petals
(800) 748-4656
www.pressedpetals.com

Prima Marketing, Inc.
(909) 627-5532
www.primamarketinginc.com

Provo Craft
(800) 937-7686
www.provocraft.com

Prym Consumer USA
www.dritz.com

PSX Design
www.sierra-enterprises.com/psxmain

Pure Scrapability
www.purescrapability.com

Purple Onion Designs
www.purpleoniondesigns.com

Queen & Co.
(858) 613-7858
www.queenandcompany.com

QuicKutz, Inc.
(888) 702-1146
www.quickutz.com

Ranger Industries, Inc.
(800) 244-2211
www.rangerink.com

Reminisce Papers
(319) 358-9777
www.shopreminisce.com

Rhonna Designs
www.rhonnadesigns.com

Royal & Langnickel/Royal Brush Mfg.
(800) 247-2211
www.royalbrush.com

Rubber Stampede
(800) 423-4135
www.rubberstampede.com

Rusty Pickle
(801) 746-1045
www.rustypickle.com

Sandylion Sticker Designs
(800) 387-4215
www.sandylion.com

Sassafras Lass
(801) 269-1331
www.sassafraslass.com

Scenic Route Paper Co.
(801) 225-5754
www.scenicroutepaper.com

Scrap Girls
(866) 598-3444
www.scrapgirls.com

ScrapArtist
(734) 717-7775
www.scrapartist.com

Scrapbook Graphics
www.scrapbookgraphics.com

ScrapDish
www.scrapdish.com

Scrapsupply
(615) 777-3953
www.scrapsupply.com

ScrapTrends
www.scraptrends.com

ScrapVillage
www.scrapvillage.com

Scrapworks, LLC /As You Wish Products, LLC
(801) 363-1010
www.scrapworks.com

SEI, Inc.
(800) 333-3279
www.shopsei.com

Shabby Princess
www.shabbyprincess.com

Shabby Shoppe, The
www.theshabbyshoppe.com

Shoebox Trims
(303) 257-7578
www.shoeboxtrims.com

Simply Clean Digi Scraps
www.simplycleanandigiscraps.com

Sizzix
(877) 355-4766
www.sizzix.com

Stampendous!
(800) 869-0474
www.stampendous.com

Stampin' Up!
(800) 782-6787
www.stampinup.com

Stamp-It
www.stampit.com.au

Staples, Inc.
www.staples.com

Stemma/Masterpiece Studios
www.masterpiecestudios.com

Sticker Studio
(888) 244-2083
www.stickerstudio.com

Stock.XCHNG
www.skc.hu

Strano Designs
(508) 454-4615
www.stranodesigns.com

Susan's Scrapbook Shack
www.susansscrapbookshack.com

Sweet Shoppe Designs
www.sweetshoppedesigns.com

Sweetwater
(800) 359-3094
www.sweetwaterscrapbook.com

Target
www.target.com

Technique Tuesday, LLC
(503) 644-4073
www.techniquetuesday.com

Three Bugs in a Rug, LLC
(801) 804-6657
www.threebugsinarug.com

Tinkering Ink
(877) 727-2784
www.tinkeringink.com

Traci Murphy Designs
www.tracimurphydesigns.com

Transparent Touches & Tags
www.transparenttouches.com

Tsukineko, Inc.
(800) 769-6633
www.tsukineko.com

Twisted Lollipop
www.twistedlollipop.com

Two Peas in a Bucket
(888) 896-7327
www.twopeasinabucket.com

Urban Lily
www.urbanlily.com

USArtQuest, Inc.
(517) 522-6225
www.usartquest.com

US Stamp & Sign
(800) 347-1044
www.usstamp.com

Wacom Technologies
(800) 922-9348
www.wacom.com

Wal-Mart Stores, Inc.
www.walmart.com

Waste Not Paper
(800) 867-2737
www.wastenotpaper.com

Watch Us, Inc.
(800) 492-8248
www.watchus.com

We R Memory Keepers, Inc.
(801) 539-5000
www.weronthenet.com

Westrim Crafts
(800) 727-2727
www.westrimcrafts.com

Wordsworth
(877) 280-0934
www.wordsworthstamps.com

WorldWin Papers
(888) 834-6455
www.worldwinpapers.com

Wrights Ribbon Accents
(877) 597-4448
www.wrights.com

Wübie Prints
(888) 256-0107
www.wubieprints.com

Xyron
(800) 793-3523
www.xyron.com

Zingboom Kits
www.zingboomkits.com

Zsiage, LLC
(718) 224-1976
www.zsiage.com

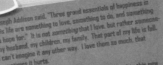

Index of Contributors

Aber, Eileen 215

Achilles, Laura 43, 75, 115, 127, 142

Adams, Yvette 82, 104, 153, 227

Albertson, Tina 60, 110

Amu, Andrea 77

Archer, Kimberly 170, 214

Armentrout, Jennifer 12, 23, 30-31

Auayfuay, Tammi 173

Austin, Krista L. 17, 62

Bartimioli, Brooke 53, 61, 64, 246

Beeson, Linda 264

Benton, Amber 216

Blanton, Susan 120

Bohl, Sara 47

Botte, Lisa 36, 135

Brouwer, Shannon 52, 127, 174, 228

Bryan, Kelly 15, 78, 172, 181, 231

Burgos, Tracy A. Weinzapfel 183

Burke, Maria 17, 32, 38, 109, 133, 143, 229, 240, 249

Callaghan, Pam 58, 252

Carroll, Lisa 54, 162, 239

Castillo, Grace 141, 206, 220, 230, 243

Cathcart, Michelle 119, 208, 215, 242

Chabot, Becky 150

Chai, Shirley 78, 133, 149

Chapman, Ann 109

Chapman, Mary Palmer 106

Christensen, Kim 14, 37, 49, 142

Cloud, Lisa 21, 203

Clouden, Francine 28, 87

Coleman, Michelle 26, 54, 68, 119, 122, 124, 130, 133-134, 138, 219

Compher, Staci 16, 115, 209, 249

Cornell, Jill 209, 256

Cutler, Amy 44, 116, 171

Davenport, Terri 186

Davies, Jane 130

Davis, Jennifer A. 146

Davis, Rachel 196

Dennis, Emily 101, 125

Dewaelsche, Heather 56, 79, 126

Dickey, Sara 14, 31

Douthit, Melanie 264

Elkins, Amy 213

Emch, Jennifer 179

Engel, Michelle 223

Fast, Alissa 235, 265

Feegel-Erhardt Catherine 108, 118, 151, 191, 198, 210, 232, 257, 261, 265

Fennell, Cari 243

Fesmire, Kathy 184, 196, 253

Fields, Sue 236

Fiero, Davinie 126

Fish, Keitha K. 195

Flaum, May 141

Fleck, Becky 93-94, 238

Ford, Summer 55, 178

Forti, Dana 192

Foster, April 59, 63, 208, 247, 254

Fowler, Kelly 213

Frantz, Kim 138

Gallacher, Jennifer S. 166, 193, 199

Gallardo-Williams, Maria 27, 117

Gallegos, Tiffany 154

Ganoe, Melita 108, 234

Geiss, Alicia 122, 222, 225

Geraghty-Groves, Jill 171, 175, 183

Goldhawk, Liz 62, 147

Greig, Rachel 29, 41, 112, 137, 227

Hagewood, Dawn 90

Hamen, Stephanie 180

Hammond, Greta 25, 64, 68, 74, 76, 85, 88, 92, 105, 162, 189-190, 232, 236, 250, 263

Harper, Nicole 13, 22, 114, 136, 139

Hassel, Charity 57, 71, 87, 172, 218

Hayes, Kellie 168

Hayes, Terri 73, 83, 114, 179, 217

Heidelberg, Hillary 34, 67, 73, 261

Heisler, Becky 163

Helmke, Stephanie A. 63

Hoel, Lisa 174

Howard, Nic 83

Hubbs, Susan 61, 107, 152

Huerta, Katrina 52, 144, 221

Hughes, Kathlynn 158

Hughes, Kim 147

Humes, Mary Anne 41, 234

Hummel, Amy 23, 134, 139, 214

Huot, Caroline 124

Inman, Wendy 59, 167, 187

Jackson-Mills, Jill 65, 199, 201-202

Jamerson, Lisa 148

Jegodtka, Roxanne 140

Johansson, Tina 69

Kajfasz, Angie 177, 183

Kelley, Julie 125

Kelley, Melissa 58, 60

Kelly, Courtney 15, 72, 129, 177, 263

Kent, Tonya Joy 35

Kisch, Lisa 128, 227

Koeppel, Amy Tara 61, 188

Korf, Nancy L. 186

Kristoff, Sue 91

Langlois, Caroline 225

Lanning, Michelle 69, 149

Leinbach, Mimi 203

Leslie, Donna 196

Liberty, Michelle Marie 107

Liu, Deborah 250

Lockett, Alison 19, 137, 257

Lokken, Karlyn 140

Long, Tanisha 70

Lontin, Carolyn A. 55

Lottermoser, Marie 48

MacAskill, Mary 120, 180, 256

Mackin, Annemarie 12, 188, 260

Mahnken, Deborah 94

Martel, Nicole 39

Martinez, Sarah 118, 125

Masters, Teri-Lynn 111

May, Shelley 200

McAndrews, Brenda 160

McElveen, Gretchen 33, 37, 43, 105, 241

McFarlin, Melanie 28, 251

Michael, Diane D. 71, 77, 260

Mikus, Wendy 98

Minchuk, Sandi 47, 106, 155, 259

Mojica, Ria 110, 176

Moreno, Kim 116, 159, 166, 220, 247

Neal, Missy 57, 225

Novacek, Becky 165, 240

O'Dell, Kelly 212

Osante, Paola López-Araiza 13, 207, 211

Osuna, Collette 36, 195

Parson, Ronee 216

Pascual, Cathy 224

Pastore, Gina 211

Perez, Carmen 113-114, 123

Peterman, Amy 45, 65, 104, 129, 131, 148, 206

Pittroff, Holly 84, 144, 223

Pixloy, Annette 184

Plantamura, Suzy 67, 97, 198, 200, 237, 248

Ploegman, Angela 212

Poelsma, Janet 131

Powell, Virginia 241

Powers, Jenny Adams 143

Prieto, Angela J. 226

Radtke, Tracie 70, 135, 194, 253

Rawlins, Crickett 207

Rieger, Crystal Jeffrey *22, 26, 32, 92, 101, 151-152, 175, 178, 217, 246, 255, 262*

Robinson, Rebekah *191*

Rogers, Kay *85, 98, 112, 117, 121, 128, 145, 151, 233*

Rogers, Mary *99-100*

Rose, Chrys Queen *219*

Rouch, Kristen Jo *257*

Saha, Mou *40, 42, 74, 132*

Salem-Lopez, Pia *181*

Schellenberg, Cathy *136, 189, 224*

Schlitzkus, Rosy *111*

Sears, Beth *79*

Severine, Champagne *19, 27, 145, 251*

Severins, Peggy *44, 191*

Sigurdson, Trudy *258*

Shimniok, Rita *87*

Simeck, Katrina *202, 235, 244*

Simon, Deborah *42*

Skinner, Michele *90, 96, 158, 161, 245*

Smit, Janneke *121*

Smith, Erika *81, 100*

Snyder, Megan *24*

Sobolewski, Linda *82*

Spell, Maureen *123, 239*

St. Clair, Michelle *25, 56*

Stanton, Sandra *18, 39, 53, 255*

Stark, Nicole *66, 88, 93, 164, 230*

Streeter, Kim *95*

Suwandi, Liana *76*

Swain, Kristen *84*

Taylor, Shannon *91, 163, 184, 248*

Teichmiller, Becky *229*

Teo, Charlene *49*

Thackston, Becky *240*

Thurman, Megan *190, 193*

Tilman, Lisa *254*

Tobey, Cindy *24, 226*

Treadaway, Tish *46, 146*

Tutman-Oglesby Lisa *20, 29, 89, 153, 182, 228, 238, 244*

Tyree, Theresa C. *221*

Valladares, Ivette *170, 185, 231, 233*

van den Ordel Edith *21*

Van Etten, Michelle *46*

van Wijck, Sarah *18, 25, 81, 168, 173, 192*

Veldman, Betsy *185*

Verrier, Heather *80, 132*

Visser, Debby *96*

Voigt, Keri *72*

Wadley, Shaunte *201*

Wagner, Matt *35*

Wahl, Janine *30, 86, 95, 160, 258*

Walker, Samantha *242, 254*

Walsh, Courtney *20, 34, 66, 159, 164, 167, 237, 245, 262*

Walter, Amanda *187*

Webster, Debbie *86*

Weibe, Andrea *45*

Weinwroth, Susan *89, 252*

Wiczling, Ariadna *40*

Wilkinson, Jody *33, 113*

Williams, Amanda *99*

Wise, Sara *80, 161, 176, 210*

Wuest, Deena *16, 38, 48, 169, 222*

Zerff, Kerry *74, 81, 165, 169, 259*

Index

4th of July *64-67*

About Me *35, 37, 40, 42-43*

Ages *54-55, 123, 138, 173, 181, 200, 202*

Amusement parks *47, 70-75, 77, 139, 200, 202*

Animals *61, 71-72, 255-259, 265*

Babies *119-120, 123, 128, 169, 174, 192, 218*

Beach *46, 78, 80-83, 110, 136, 150, 188*

Beauty *108-109, 111-112, 121, 129, 142*

Bicycles *26-27, 130, 138, 186, 191*

Birthdays *52-55*

Body parts *16, 18, 21-22, 111, 142, 180, 182, 201*

Boys *158-203*

Bugs *150-151, 172*

Children *16-17, 104-155, 158-203, 218-222, 224-227, 238-243*

Christmas *92-97*

Couples *206-216*

Dads *217, 229-230, 232-233, 236-237, 254*

Dance *153*

Daughters and sons *219-222, 224-227*

Dress-up *104, 122, 126, 162, 178, 223*

Easter *57-59*

Fall *84-87, 160*

Family *32, 233, 254*

Fashion *30, 104, 106-107*

Favorite things *76, 134, 202-203*

First steps *132*

Flowers *44, 60, 62*

Food *24-25, 67, 73, 140, 164, 200*

Friends *244-245, 260-265*

Girls *104-155*

Grandparents *246-253*

Hair *23, 109, 163*

Halloween *88-91, 104*

Happy *49, 112, 117, 128, 136, 140, 155*

Laughter *65, 108, 123, 173*

Life *37, 45-46*

Moms *29-30, 33, 219, 228-229, 231-232, 234-236, 254*

Money *22, 160*

Museums *70*

Names *120, 122, 128, 131, 146-147, 173-174, 180, 182, 187, 218*

Parties *27, 144*

Pets *255-259*

Photography *12-14, 124-125, 164*

Play *17, 21, 69, 143, 161, 179, 185, 193*

Reading *135*

Rock 'n' roll *149, 198*

School *132-133, 166, 168, 190, 202*

Shopping *76-77*

Siblings *16-17, 218-221, 238-246*

Smiles *112, 116, 124, 170, 175*

Sports *26, 152, 194-197*

Spring *117*

Summer *68, 73-74, 76, 78, 81, 159*

Talking *105, 109, 145, 166, 176*

Tools *28*

Tooth fairy *20*

Toys *127, 139, 158, 167*

Trouble *162*

Vacation *74, 78-79, 81-83, 254*

Valentine's Day *56*

Water *68-69, 81, 147, 184, 188-189, 198*

Weddings *63, 207, 210*

Wheels *144, 184, 186-187, 191, 193*

Winter *98-99, 100-101, 199*

Wishes *48-49, 53, 146, 155, 183*

Get more scrapbook inspiration from these Memory Makers books!

That's Life

Popular scrapbook designer Nic Howard teaches you how to identify, capture and chronicle everyday moments and daily routines in your scrapbook pages.

ISBN-13: 978-1-59963-001-4
ISBN-10: 1-59963-001-X
paperback
112 pages

Z0689

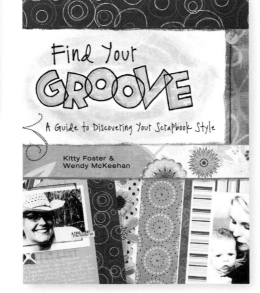

Find Your Groove

Kitty Foster and Wendy McKeehan take you on a journey to discovering your own groovy scrapbook style through quizzes, exercises, challenges and page after page of fabulous layouts sure to inspire.

ISBN-13: 978-1-59963-006-9
ISBN-10: 1-59963-006-0
paperback
112 pages

Z0787

These books and other fine Memory Makers titles are available at your local craft or scrapbook store, bookstore or from online suppliers, including *www.memorymakersmagazine.com.*

Travel Scrapbooks

Discover creative ways to organize vacation photos into mini-albums featuring your favorite travel destinations.

ISBN-13: 978-1-59963-008-3
ISBN-10: 1-59963-008-7
paperback
128 pages

Z0789

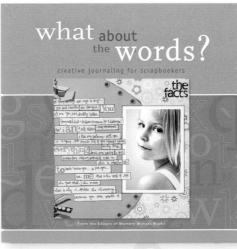

What About the Words?

Journaling on your scrapbook layouts is easy with the advice, examples and inspirations found here.

ISBN-13: 978-1-892127-77-8
ISBN-10: 1-892127-77-6
paperback
128 pages

Z0017

See what's coming up from Memory Makers Books by checking out our blog: *www.memorymakersmagazine.com/booksblog/*